The FADE OUT

IMAGE COMICS, INC.
Robert Kirkman - Chief Operating Officer
Erik Larsen - Chief Financial Officer
Todd McFarlane - President
Marc Silvestri - Chief Executive Officer
Jim Valentino - Vice-President
Eric Stephenson - Publisher
Corey Murphy - Director of Sales
Jeff Boison - Director of Publishing Planning
& Book Trade Sales
Jeremy Sullivan - Director of Digital Sales
Kat Salazar - Director of PR & Marketing
Emily Miller - Director of Operations
Branwyn Bigglestone - Senior Accounts Manager
Sarah Mello - Accounts Manager

Drew Gill - Art Director
Jonathan Chan - Production Manager
Meredith Wallace - Print Manager
Briah Skelly - Publicity Assistant
Randy Okamura - Marketing Production Designer
David Brothers - Branding Manager
Ally Power - Content Manager
Addison Duke - Production Artist
Vincent Kukua - Production Artist
Sasha Head - Production Artist
Tricia Ramos - Production Artist
Jeff Stang - Direct Market Sales Representative
Emilio Bautista - Digital Sales Associate
Chloe Ramos-Peterson - Administrative Assistant
IMAGECOMICS.COM

Thanks to Amy Condit.

Editorial Coordinator: Sebastian Girner.

THE FADE OUT: ACT THREE. First printing. February 2016. Contains material originally published in magazine form as THE FADE OUT #9-12.

ISBN: 978-1-63215-629-7

 Publication design by Sean Phillips

the FADE OUT

Ed Brubaker
Sean Phillips
Colors by
Elizabeth Breitweiser

Act Three

CHARLIE PARISH
Screenwriter for a Blacklisted
Friend

GIL MASON
Blacklisted Screenwriter

PHIL BRODSKY
Studio Security Chief

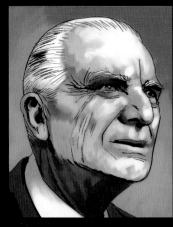

MELBA MASON
Gil's Amazing Wife

VICTOR THURSBY
Co-Founder of Victory Street
Pictures

DOTTIE QUINN
Studio PR Girl

FRANZ SCHMITT
German Expatriate Director

EARL RATH
Dashing Leading Man

DRAKE MILLER
A Big Question Mark

Living in a Memory

CHARLIE HADN'T BEEN TO THE HOUSE IN YEARS.

DROPPING BY AT MIDNIGHT ON *HALLOWEEN* PROBABLY WOULDN'T BE APPRECIATED.

BUT HE DIDN'T CARE...

HE WAS TOO BUSY WORRYING ABOUT HOW FUCKED HE WAS.

HOW FUCKED *THEY* WERE.

CHARLIE...? IS THAT YOU?

WHAT ARE YOU *DOING*?

IT'S THE MIDDLE OF THE NIGHT...

SORRY, I TRIED TO BE QUIET...

JUST NEED TO *GET* SOMETHING AND I'LL BE OUT OF YOUR HAIR...

YOU CAN'T JUST *COME* BY LIKE THIS.

WHY NOT? I *PAID* FOR THIS HOUSE.

HE REGRETS SAYING IT THE *SECOND* THE WORDS LEAVE HIS MOUTH.

JESUS, CHARLIE...

IT WAS ALWAYS LIKE THAT WITH HIM AND REBECCA...

HE NEVER GOT IT RIGHT.

WE ALL THOUGHT YOU WERE DEAD...

THEY SENT ME A TELEGRAM.

GUESS THEY DIDN'T *KNOW* ABOUT THE DIVORCE...

BUT THEY SAY YOU'RE GOING TO BE FINE.

THE DOCTOR TOLD ME IT'S JUST *FATIGUE*.

EVEN STAYING SILENT...

TO SPARE HER MISERY SHE DOESN'T *REALLY* WANT TO KNOW ABOUT...

EVEN *THAT* WAS THE WRONG THING TO DO.

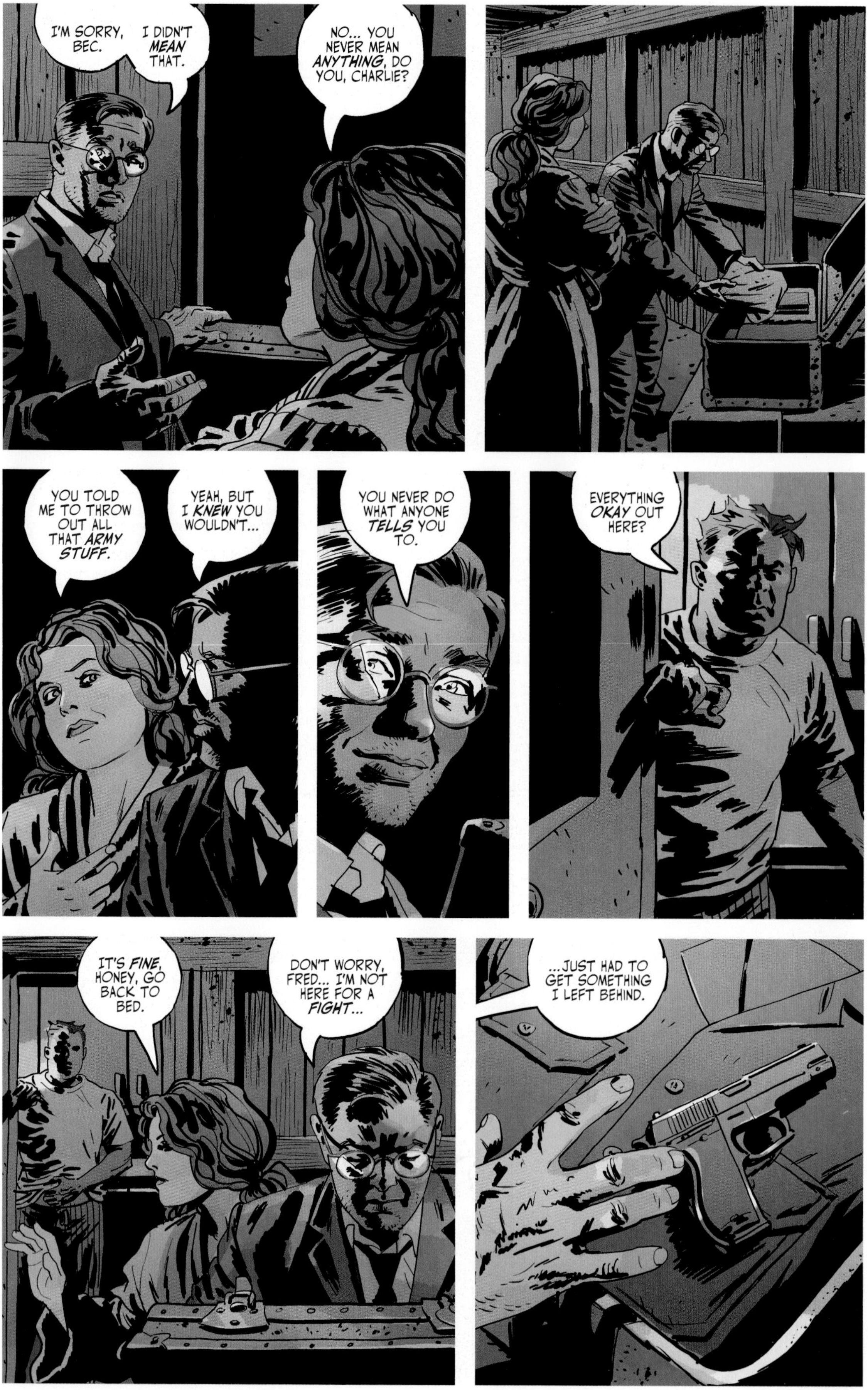
I'M SORRY, BEC.
I DIDN'T MEAN THAT.
NO... YOU NEVER MEAN ANYTHING, DO YOU, CHARLIE?
YOU TOLD ME TO THROW OUT ALL THAT ARMY STUFF.
YEAH, BUT I KNEW YOU WOULDN'T...
YOU NEVER DO WHAT ANYONE TELLS YOU TO.
EVERYTHING OKAY OUT HERE?
IT'S FINE, HONEY, GO BACK TO BED.
DON'T WORRY, FRED... I'M NOT HERE FOR A FIGHT...
...JUST HAD TO GET SOMETHING I LEFT BEHIND.

THE GUN DOESN'T SETTLE HIS NERVES...

BUT HE'S STILL GLAD TO HAVE IT.

CHARLIE HAD SEEN VIOLENT MEN IN ACTION TOO MANY TIMES...

Better get somewhere *safe*... Looks like they're here.

TROUBLE BOYS... AND SOLDIERS...

IN THE REAL WORLD, IT WASN'T EXCITING OR CINEMATIC.

What are you going to *do*, Bill?

Nothing I want you to *see*, baby doll.

WOULD HE EVEN BE ABLE TO PULL THE TRIGGER IF THEY CAME FOR HIM?

WAS HE THAT MUCH OF A SURVIVOR...?

SHIT...

OH... HEY, CHARLIE...

DIDN'T THINK YOU'D BE HERE...

HEY... WHOA -- IS...?

If you don't want the truth about Valeria Sommers death to come out, put $1000 dollars in a ba gg

WHAT'RE YOU DOIN' WITH A GUN, CHARLIE?

YOU STUPID SON OF A BITCH...

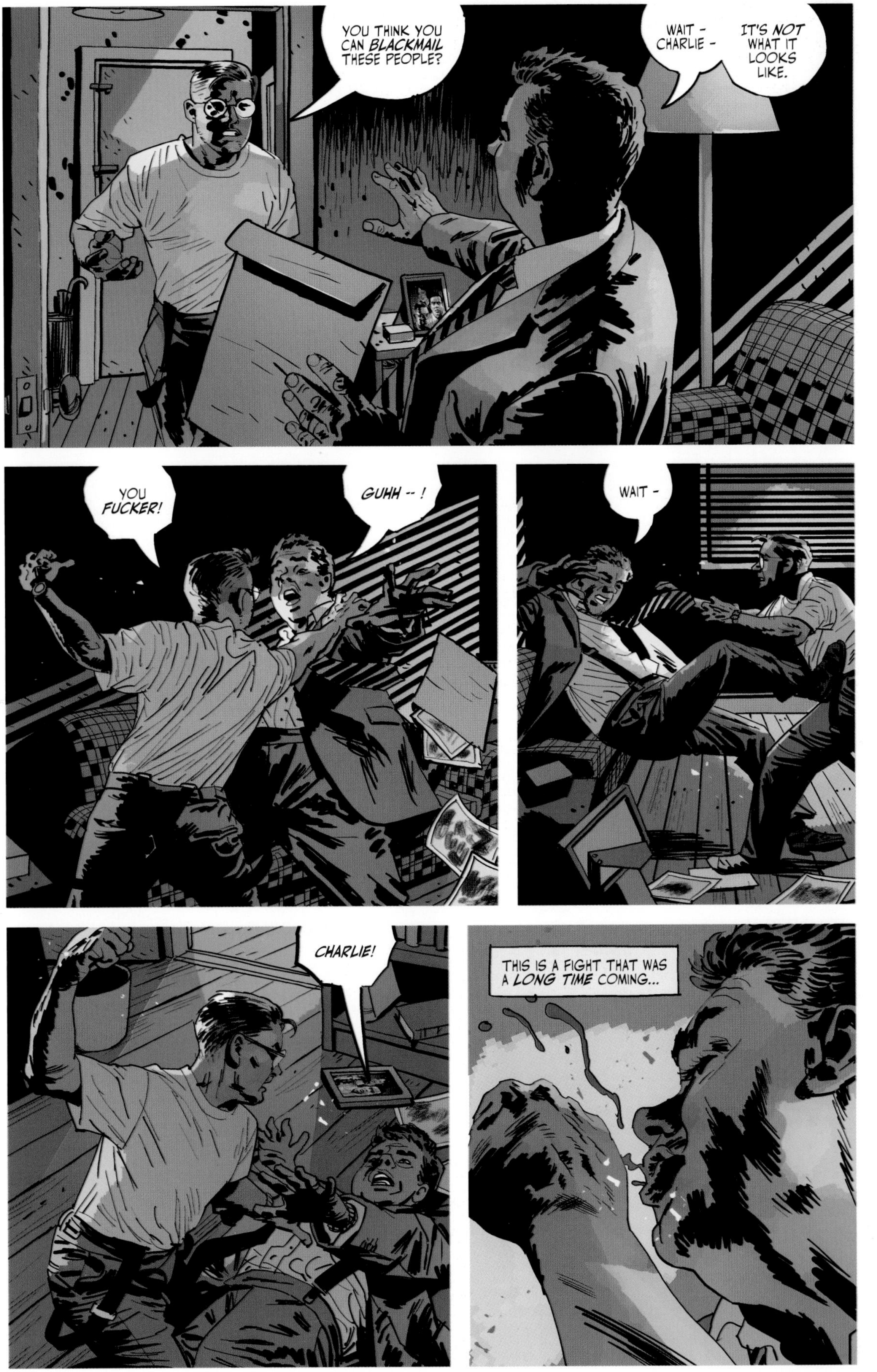
YOU THINK YOU CAN BLACKMAIL THESE PEOPLE?
WAIT - CHARLIE -
IT'S NOT WHAT IT LOOKS LIKE.
YOU FUCKER!
GUHH -- !
WAIT -
CHARLIE!
THIS IS A FIGHT THAT WAS A LONG TIME COMING...

BUT TO UNDERSTAND THAT, YOU HAVE TO UNDERSTAND THE DEPTH OF CHARLIE AND GIL'S FRIENDSHIP...

AND HOW THEY WERE BOUND TOGETHER BY THE KIND OF WOUNDS *USUALLY* INFLICTED ONLY ON FAMILY.

GIL HAD COME TO HOLLYWOOD OFF THE BACK OF A *NOVEL* THAT SOLD ONLY A FEW THOUSAND COPIES...

BUT THE CRITICS SAID HE HAD A "VOICE" AND THAT WAS WHAT THE *STUDIOS* WANTED.

HE WAS *ALMOST* ENOUGH OF A HAYSEED TO BELIEVE IT...

BUT WHEN HE ARRIVED AT *MGM* IN 1937...

...HIS FIRST ASSIGNMENT WAS TO REWRITE HIS FAVORITE AUTHOR.

Oct. 1937 revision

by

F. Scott Fitzgerald

AND NEITHER OF THEM GOT *CREDIT* ON THE FILM WHEN IT WAS RELEASED.

BY THE TIME HE MET CHARLIE, GIL HAD VERY FEW ILLUSIONS ABOUT THE MOVIE BUSINESS...

IT'S A *RACKET*, KID... AND WRITERS LIKE YOU AND ME...

FAR AS THE *BOSSES* ARE CONCERNED, WE'RE A DIME A DOZEN...

THIS TOWN'S FULL TO THE BRIM WITH FRESH YOUNG IDIOTS JUST *WAITING* TO TAKE YOUR JOB.

YEAH, SURE... BUT IT'S STILL THE *PICTURES*, GIL...

DOESN'T THAT GET YOU SMILING *AT ALL*?

AHH, CHARLIE... SO NAÏVE...

STILL, THERE WAS SOMETHING *INFECTIOUS* ABOUT THE KID'S AMBITION...

AND GIL FOUND HIMSELF GIVING A SHIT AGAIN FOR THE FIRST TIME IN YEARS.

THE SCRIPTS HE WROTE THAT YEAR, WHEN THEY SHARED THAT LITTLE OFFICE AT *RKO*...

THOSE WERE THE BEST THINGS GIL *EVER* WROTE.

THEY JUST WEREN'T AS GOOD AS WHAT *CHARLIE* WAS DOING...

YOU SONNOVA BITCH – A FUCKING *OSCAR* NOMINATION!

CONGRATS, PAL!

AHH, IT'S JUST *LUCK*...

AND Y'KNOW, YOU *FIXED* THAT SECOND ACT FOR ME...

IT WAS A *MESS.*

ENOUGH OF THE *MODESTY* CRAP, CHARLIE.

I'M *HAPPY* FOR YOU...

AND HE *WAS*... GIL WAS HAPPY FOR HIS FRIEND...

NOW C'MON, WE'RE PAINTING THE TOWN...

BUT SOMEWHERE AROUND THE FIFTH DRINK, HIS *ENVY* CAME CREEPING IN...

AND HE *HATED* HIMSELF FOR FEELING THAT WAY, EVEN FOR A SECOND.

MAYBE *THAT'S* WHY THE NIGHT WENT WRONG, BECAUSE HE WAS *MAD* AT HIMSELF...

DEAL ME *IN*, FELLAS...

OR MAYBE GIL WAS JUST A *TROUBLE-MAGNET*, LIKE CHARLIE ALWAYS SAID.

BUT EITHER WAY, THE NIGHT WENT WRONG.

JESUS H CHRIST... HOW STUPID *ARE* YOU TWO...?

DON'T YOU *KNOW* WHO OWNS THIS JOINT?

I KNOW IT'S NOBODY *LEGIT*...

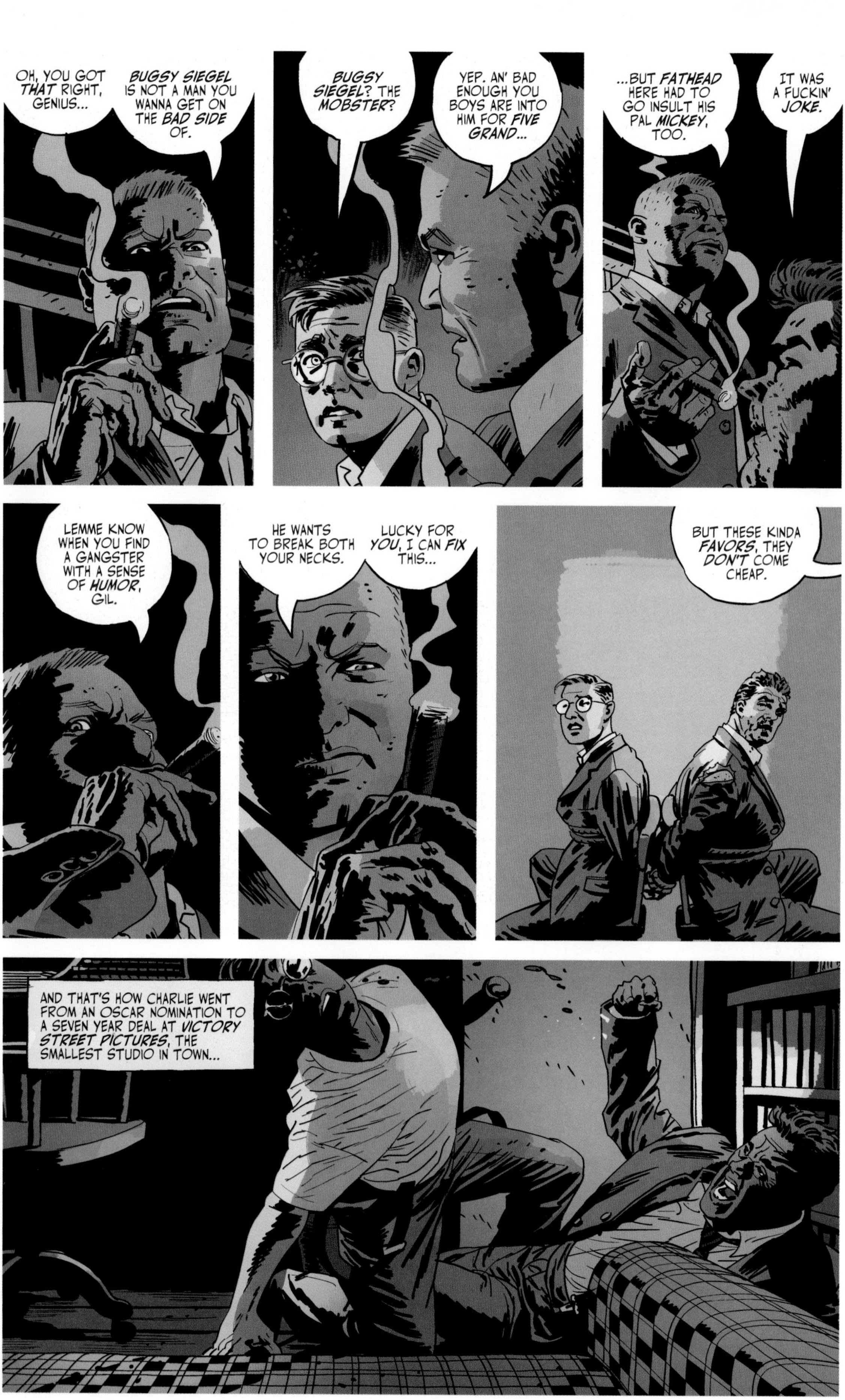
OH, YOU GOT THAT RIGHT, GENIUS...
BUGSY SIEGEL IS NOT A MAN YOU WANNA GET ON THE BAD SIDE OF.
BUGSY SIEGEL? THE MOBSTER?
YEP. AN' BAD ENOUGH YOU BOYS ARE INTO HIM FOR FIVE GRAND...
...BUT FATHEAD HERE HAD TO GO INSULT HIS PAL MICKEY, TOO.
IT WAS A FUCKIN' JOKE.
LEMME KNOW WHEN YOU FIND A GANGSTER WITH A SENSE OF HUMOR, GIL.
HE WANTS TO BREAK BOTH YOUR NECKS.
LUCKY FOR YOU, I CAN FIX THIS...
BUT THESE KINDA FAVORS, THEY DON'T COME CHEAP.
AND THAT'S HOW CHARLIE WENT FROM AN OSCAR NOMINATION TO A SEVEN YEAR DEAL AT VICTORY STREET PICTURES, THE SMALLEST STUDIO IN TOWN...

THIS WAS THE COST OF THEIR BOND...

THEIR SHARED SPIRAL DOWN THE BOOZE-HOLE.

CHARLIE AND GIL BARELY SPOKE FOR THE REST OF THAT YEAR... UNTIL *PEARL HARBOR.*

HOLDING A GRUDGE FELT *PETTY* IN THE FACE OF WAR...

I'M REALLY *SORRY,* PAL.

IT'S OKAY...

I KNEW WHO I WAS GOING *DRINKING WITH,* GIL.

WE ARE WHO WE *ARE...*

WELL, HOW ABOUT I GET THE *NEXT ROUND,* ANYWAY?

DEAL.

CHARLIE'S WIFE WOULD LEAVE HIM A FEW WEEKS LATER...

AND NOT LONG AFTER *THAT*, HE'D BE ON HIS WAY TO ENGLAND, TO SEE THE WAR *UP CLOSE*...

AND FIND OUT HOW SMALL IT MADE *EVERYTHING* FEEL.

GIL BARELY RECOGNIZED HIM WHEN THEY PICKED HIM UP FROM THE *HOSPITAL*...

GREAT TO SEE YOU, PAL.

YEAH... SURE... THANKS...

THE SUMMER OF '45 THEY SAW SO MANY SOLDIERS RETURNING HOME... GLASSY-EYED AND LOST...

SOME WITH *LIMBS* OR *EYES* MISSING...

OTHERS LIKE CHARLIE, MISSING THINGS YOU COULDN'T SEE.

MAYBE THAT'S WHY GIL NEVER BLAMED HIM FOR *HIS PART* IN THEIR TANGLED MESS.

OR MAYBE IT WAS BECAUSE NO ONE COULD BE *BLAMED* FOR LOVING SOMEONE.

THAT WAS CERTAINLY HOW *MELBA* SAW IT.

THERE WAS SO MUCH LIQUOR FLOWING THROUGH THEIR HOUSE THOSE MONTHS... AS THEY TRIED TO BRING CHARLIE BACK TO *LIFE.*

INHIBITIONS JUST FELL AWAY...

WAIT... WE CAN'T...

WE ALREADY *ARE,* CHARLIE...

BUT... WE *SHOULDN'T*...

GIL DOESN'T *OWN* ME.

IT'S OKAY TO FEEL *GOOD*, CHARLIE...

THERE'S STILL LOVE FOR YOU IN THIS WORLD.

CHARLIE HAD SEEN GIL WITH OTHER WOMEN, BUT NOW HE REALIZED IT WAS WITH MELBA'S PERMISSION.

THIS IS WHY GIL HAD FALLEN IN LOVE WITH HER, SHE WAS LIKE A CHARACTER OUT OF A *FITZGERALD* NOVEL...

UNDERSTANDING HOW FRAGILE AND FLAWED PEOPLE WERE...

KNOWING THAT YOU DIDN'T NEED TO PUNISH THEM FOR THAT.

AND MAYBE GIL WOULDN'T HAVE CARED, IF HE HADN'T WOKEN UP.

BUT CHARLIE WILL NEVER FORGET GIL'S CONFUSED EYES STARING INTO THE DARKNESS...

WATCHING HIS WIFE MAKE LOVE TO HIS BEST FRIEND.

GIL'S *TAILSPIN* STARTED SOON AFTER THAT.

DRUNKEN FIGHTS AT PARTIES...

YELLING AT STUDIO BOSSES OVER CONTRACTS...

AND FINALLY CRASHING LIKE A KAMIKAZE PILOT BEFORE THE *HOUSE COMMITTEE.*

IT WAS LIKE A SLOW-MOTION SUICIDE, AND NO MATTER WHAT MELBA SAID, CHARLIE FELT RESPONSIBLE.

THESE WERE THE SINS THEY'D BOTH FORGIVEN, THAT NEVER REALLY WENT AWAY.

THE SHARED BLAME OF RUINED LIVES.

DO YOU EVEN *KNOW* WHAT YOU'VE DONE...?

SCREW YOU...

VAL WAS YOUR *FRIEND* AND YOU WERE GONNA LET THIS WHOLE THING *DROP.*

NO, I *WASN'T.* I WAS JUST...

HEY...?

GIL...? WHAT *IS* THIS?

YOU *KNOW* WHAT IT IS...

JESUS, GIL... THIS...

WHAT THE *FUCK* DID YOU DO?

SAID IT WASN'T WHAT IT LOOKED LIKE... I WASN'T *BLACKMAILING* THEM...

I WAS TRYING TO SEE WHAT THEY'D *DO* IF THEY THOUGHT SOMEONE WAS *ONTO* THEM.

"AND IT WORKED... OLD MAN THURSBY WAS CLEARLY *SPOOKED* BY MY FIRST LETTER...

"HE DIDN'T GO TO THE *STUDIO* THAT DAY.

"INSTEAD HE GOT HIS *DRIVER* TO TAKE HIM INTO HOLLYWOOD..."

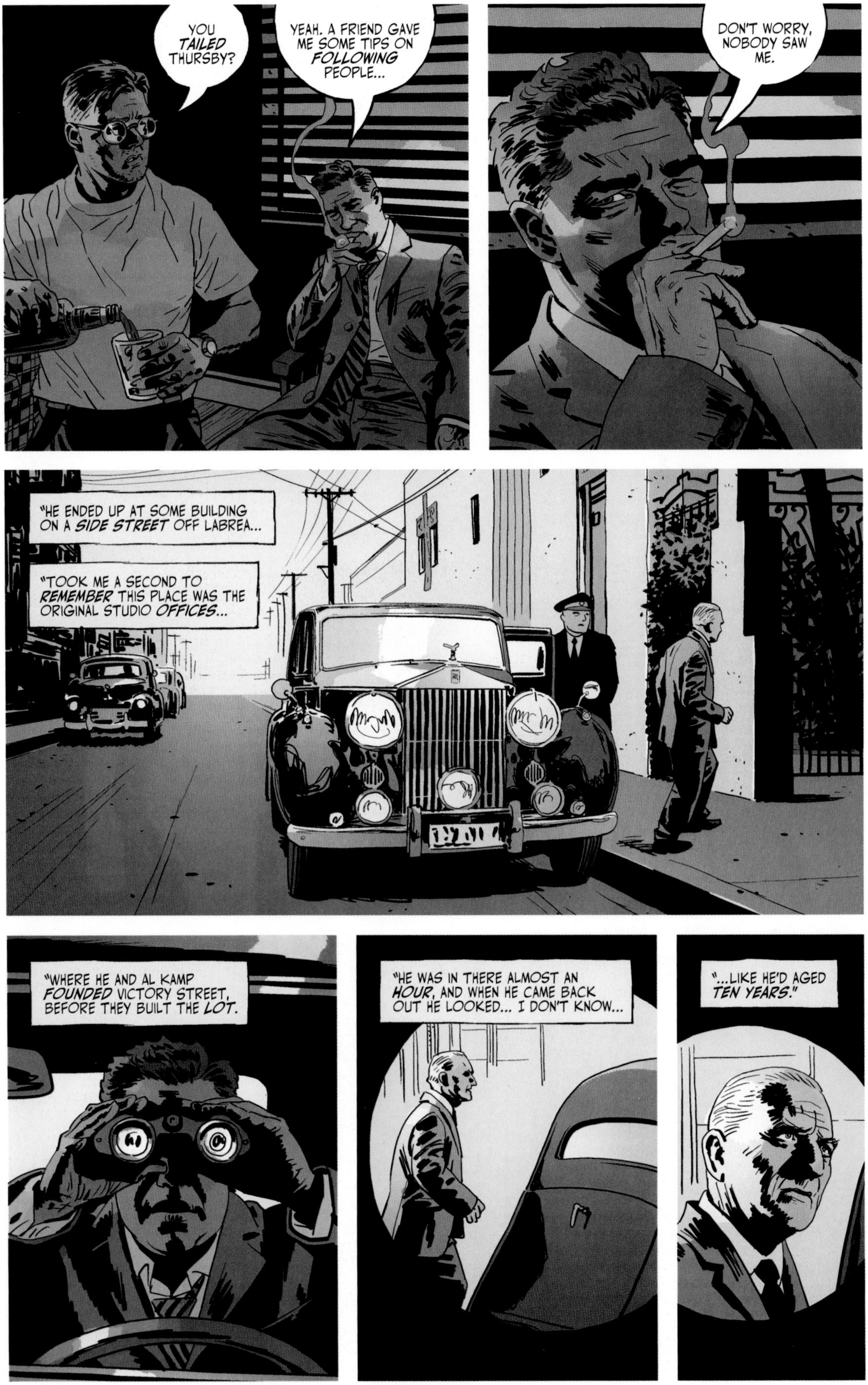
YOU TAILED THURSBY?
YEAH. A FRIEND GAVE ME SOME TIPS ON FOLLOWING PEOPLE...
DON'T WORRY, NOBODY SAW ME.
"HE ENDED UP AT SOME BUILDING ON A SIDE STREET OFF LABREA...
"TOOK ME A SECOND TO REMEMBER THIS PLACE WAS THE ORIGINAL STUDIO OFFICES...
"WHERE HE AND AL KAMP FOUNDED VICTORY STREET, BEFORE THEY BUILT THE LOT.
"HE WAS IN THERE ALMOST AN HOUR, AND WHEN HE CAME BACK OUT HE LOOKED... I DON'T KNOW...
"...LIKE HE'D AGED TEN YEARS."

"AFTER HE *LEFT*, I PRETENDED TO BE LOOKING FOR AN OFFICE RENTAL...

"AND THE SECURITY GUARD TOLD ME THE BUILDING'S MOSTLY A *STORAGE HOUSE* FOR THE STUDIO NOW.

"PLACE HAS *FILM VAULTS* ON EVERY FLOOR."

SEE? YOU *SCARE* THESE GUYS AN' THEY RUN TO MAKE SURE THEIR *ASSES* ARE COVERED...

IS *THAT* HOW YOU GOT THE PICTURES, YOU *BROKE-IN* THERE?

NO... HELL WITH *THAT*...

THAT *GUARD* DIDN'T SEEM LIKE HE'D *MIND* SHOOTING A BURGLAR.

NO, I FOLLOWED *BRODSKY* THE NEXT FEW DAYS INSTEAD.

HE WAS DRIVIN' ALL OVER TOWN, GETTING *ANGRIER* WITH EVERY STOP HE MADE...

"BUT IT WASN'T 'TIL MY *SECOND* LETTER, ASKING FOR *MONEY*, THAT IT GOT REALLY INTERESTING..."

"BEFORE HE WENT TO MAKE THE *DROP* TONIGHT, BRODSKY MET WITH A FEW OF HIS *GUYS*."

"I KNEW WHERE *HE'D* BE, SO I TAILED *THEM* THIS TIME..."

"AND THEY WENT *RIGHT* TO THE SAME PLACE *THURSBY* LED ME TO."

"COUPLE MINUTES LATER, THEY'RE HAULING OUT *FILE BOXES*..."

"THEN THEY DRIVE OUT TO THE BEACH AND START *BURNING* EVERYTHING."

"I DON'T KNOW *WHAT* I WAS EXPECTING TO FIND, BUT IT WASN'T *THIS...*"

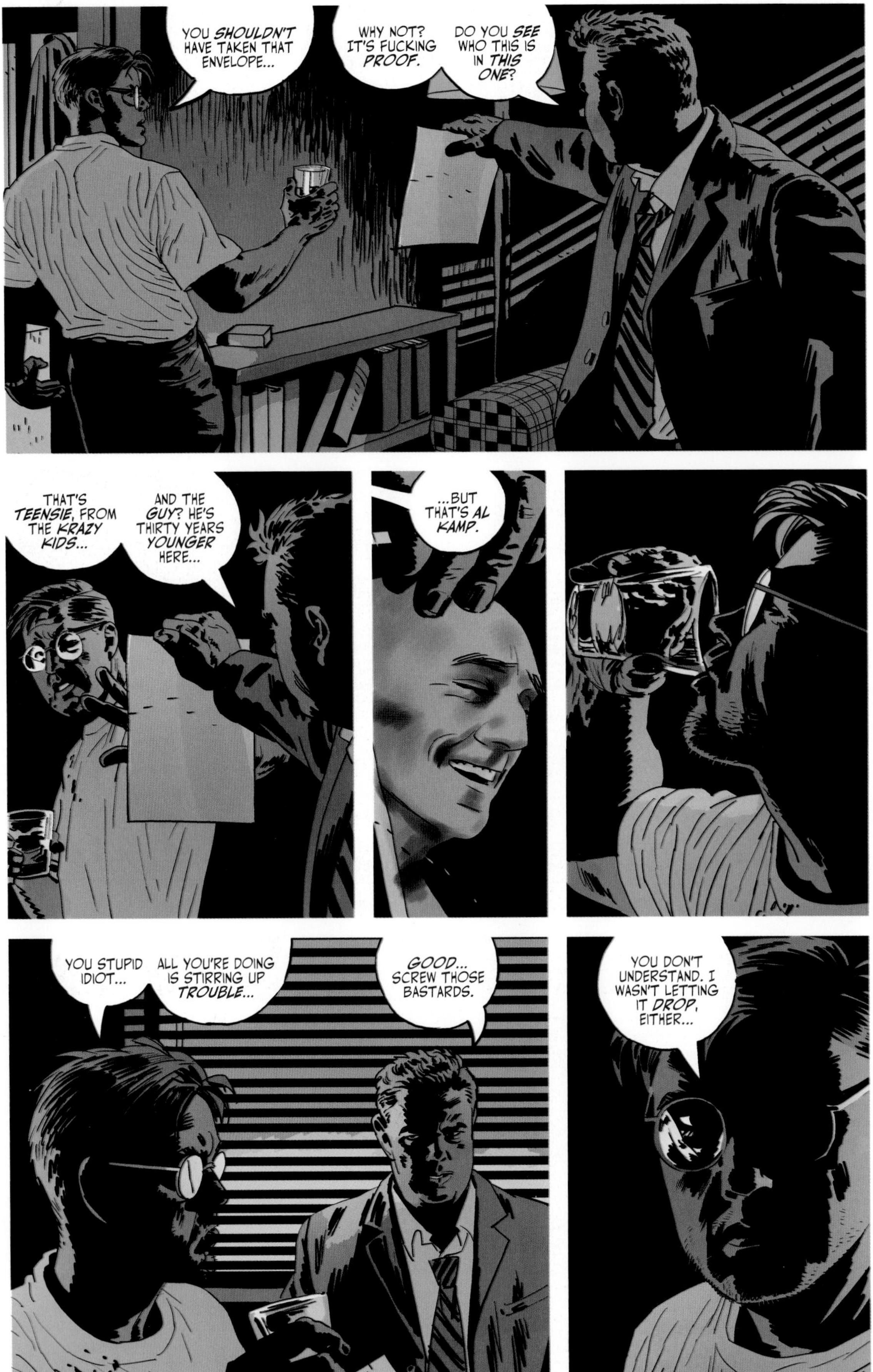
YOU SHOULDN'T HAVE TAKEN THAT ENVELOPE...
WHY NOT? IT'S FUCKING PROOF.
DO YOU SEE WHO THIS IS IN THIS ONE?
THAT'S TEENSIE, FROM THE KRAZY KIDS...
AND THE GUY? HE'S THIRTY YEARS YOUNGER HERE...
...BUT THAT'S AL KAMP.
YOU STUPID IDIOT...
ALL YOU'RE DOING IS STIRRING UP TROUBLE...
GOOD... SCREW THOSE BASTARDS.
YOU DON'T UNDERSTAND. I WASN'T LETTING IT DROP, EITHER...

AND AS OF TONIGHT, MY MAIN SUSPECTS ARE AN FBI *FRONT MAN*...

...AND *EARL FUCKING RATH*.

WHAT? *EARL*...?

THAT'S RIGHT... AND BRODSKY'S *ONE STEP AWAY* FROM FINDING OUT WHERE I *WAS* WHEN VAL DIED.

HOW LONG DO YOU THINK IT'LL TAKE HIM TO FIGURE OUT WHO'S *BLACKMAILING* THEM AFTER THAT?

I DON'T KNOW. LONG ENOUGH TO GET THESE *PICTURES* TO THE PAPERS.

YOU THINK THEY DON'T *OWN* THE *PAPERS*?

WE CAN'T *WIN* AGAINST THESE GUYS.

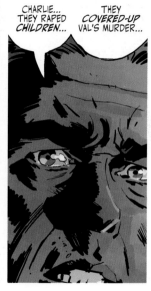

CHARLIE... THEY RAPED *CHILDREN*...

THEY *COVERED-UP* VAL'S MURDER...

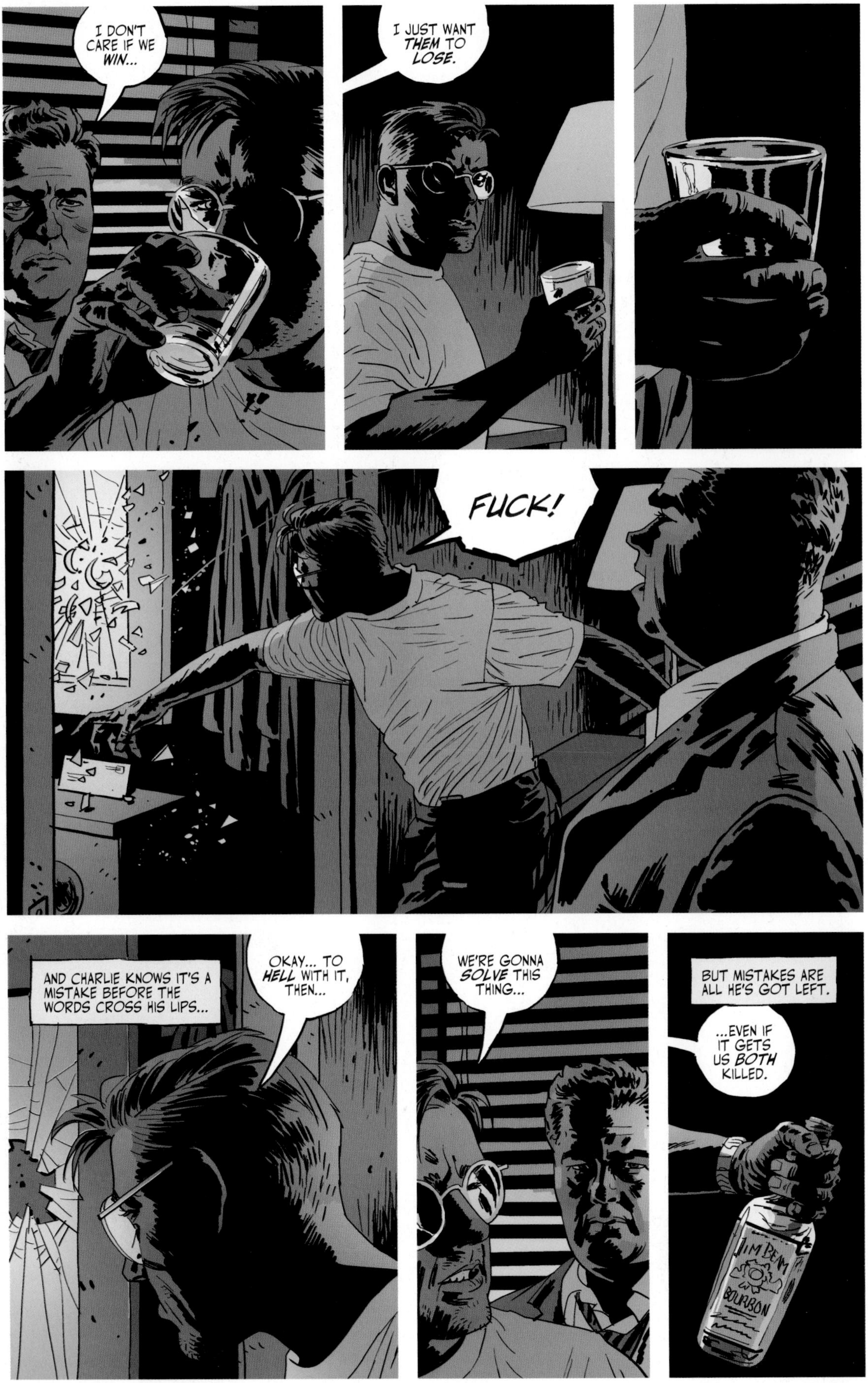
I DON'T CARE IF WE WIN...
I JUST WANT THEM TO LOSE.
FUCK!
AND CHARLIE KNOWS IT'S A MISTAKE BEFORE THE WORDS CROSS HIS LIPS...
OKAY... TO HELL WITH IT, THEN...
WE'RE GONNA SOLVE THIS THING...
BUT MISTAKES ARE ALL HE'S GOT LEFT.
...EVEN IF IT GETS US BOTH KILLED.
JIM BEAM
BOURBON

Where Angels Fear to Tread

DOTTIE WAS *ALREADY* LATE TO THE WRAP PARTY...

NO, I HADN'T *HEARD* THAT... *JOHN GARFIELD?*

BUT SOMETIMES YOU COULDN'T GET *HEDDA HOPPER* OFF THE PHONE...

ISN'T HE A *JEW*, THOUGH?

ESPECIALLY WHEN SHE STARTED TALKING ABOUT *COMMIES*.

I DON'T KNOW... JUST BECAUSE HE SIGNED THAT *FIRST AMENDMENT* THING?

I MEAN, SO DID *BOGIE*...

UH HUNH... HMM...

ANYHOW... CAN WE SET A *TIME* FOR YOUR VISIT WITH *TYLER?*

NO NO... HE'S *STILL* GORGEOUS. YOU'LL *SEE.*

AND IT'S AN *EXCLUSIVE* -- LOUELLA WON'T EVEN KNOW HE'S GETTING *RELEASED* UNTIL SHE READS IT IN *YOUR* COLUMN.

SOMETIMES SHE COULDN'T BELIEVE THIS WAS HER JOB.

HELPING ACTORS KEEP SECRETS... REWRITING THEIR HISTORY...

MAKING BEAUTIFUL PEOPLE EVEN MORE SEDUCTIVE...

ALL SO JOHN Q. PUBLIC WOULDN'T SEE WHO THEY REALLY WERE.

BUT DOTTIE HAD LEARNED LONG AGO THE WORLD DIDN'T REALLY WANT TO KNOW THE TRUTH ABOUT *ANYONE*.

TYLER GRA

THEY'D ALWAYS RATHER HAVE A STORY.

I'VE GOT TO DROP THIS AT *BRODSKY'S* OFFICE, THEN I'M HEADING TO THE PARTY... SEE YOU *THERE?*

SURE...

PUBLICITY DEPT

SHE'D BEEN MAKING UP STORIES ABOUT *HERSELF* MOST OF HER LIFE, SO SHE KNEW HOW IT WORKED.

PUBLIC
DEP

DOTTIE KNEW THE *POWER* OF SECRETS AND HOW TO *KEEP* THEM.

BUT NOT EVERYONE WAS LIKE HER... OR PHIL BRODSKY WOULDN'T HAVE SO MANY *FIRES* TO PUT OUT.

NO. WITH MOST PEOPLE, SECRETS BURNED INSIDE THEM... FIGHTING TO GET OUT...

CHARLIE?

AH... *SHIT.*

WHAT IN *GOD'S NAME* ARE YOU *UP* TO?

SHIT... I DIDN'T WANNA *INVOLVE* YOU...

BUT I GUESS WE BETTER *TALK.*

SOUNDS SERIOUS...

ALL RIGHT, MASKED MAN, LET'S GO FIND SOMEWHERE *PRIVATE...*

GIL AND CHARLIE HAD SPENT DAYS ARGUING ABOUT WHAT TO DO NEXT...

WOULD YOU JUST *LISTEN* TO ME?

HELL *NO* -- YOU'VE ALREADY MADE *TOO MANY* MISTAKES.

THOSE PHOTOS HAD GIL ALL *TORN-UP* INSIDE...

SO ALL *HE* WANTED TO DO WAS GO AFTER *OLD MAN KAMP*.

YOU DON'T *GET IT*, CHARLIE... HE'S FUCKING SENILE.

WHEN I SAW HIM THAT NIGHT IN *OJAI*...

BRODSKY WASN'T WORRIED ABOUT SOMETHING *HAPPENING* TO THE OLD MAN...

HE WAS WORRIED I'D *TALKED* TO HIM.

BECAUSE KAMP DOESN'T EVEN *KNOW* WHAT HE'S SAYING ANYMORE.

WE GET HIM ALONE FOR FIVE MINUTES, WE'LL KNOW *EVERYTHING*...

BUT CHARLIE HAD OTHER IDEAS.

BEFORE WE EVEN *THINK* ABOUT THAT, WE NEED TO KNOW WHAT *HAPPENED* THAT NIGHT...

IT'S *CONNECTED* TO KAMP. IT'S *GOTTA* BE.

KAMP *WASN'T THERE* WHEN VAL GOT KILLED...

THEN WHY ARE THEY CLEANING UP *HIS MESS* ALL OF A SUDDEN?

MAYBE BECAUSE YOU STIRRED UP A HORNET'S NEST.

I'M TELLING YOU, THESE *SONS OF BITCHES* --

ENOUGH.

THIS ISN'T ABOUT THE *FAT CATS* WHO WRECKED YOUR LIFE...

IT'S ABOUT *HER.*

THOSE MISSING HOURS IN HIS MIND...

THE *BLANK SPOTS* WHERE VAL LOST EVERYTHING A GIRL CAN LOSE...

THAT WAS THE WEIGHT PROPELLING CHARLIE NOW.

AND HE COULDN'T SHRUG IT OFF AGAIN...

NO, HE WOULDN'T.

ALL RIGHT... WE DO IT *YOUR WAY* FOR NOW...

BUT HOW THE HELL DO WE *FIND OUT* ABOUT THAT NIGHT?

IT TOOK CHARLIE A MOMENT TO REALIZE IT...

BUT THERE WAS ACTUALLY A *SIMPLE ANSWER* TO THAT.

BRODSKY.

BRODSKY HAD BEEN DIGGING INTO THAT NIGHT EVER SINCE GIL STARTED SENDING *BLACKMAIL* THREATS...

THE STUDIO HAD *COVERED-UP* VAL'S MURDER AND HE NEEDED TO MAKE SURE IT *STAYED* THAT WAY.

RNNNGG

THAT'S WHAT *FIXERS* DID.

BRODSKY...

BUT THEY ALSO KEPT RECORDS, TO BE USED FOR *LEVERAGE.*

WHAT THE FUCK DID YOU JUST *SAY?*

I SAID YOU *BLEW IT,* ASSHOLE. I WAS GONNA LET YOU OFF *EASY...*

BUT YOU STUCK AROUND... TRIED TO *CATCH* ME WITH MY HAND IN THE *COOKIE JAR.*

SO SCREW *YOU,* TOUGH GUY.

NOW THE PRICE IS *TWENTY GRAND*...

BRODSKY'S *FILES* WERE LEGENDARY.

SECRETS, PICTURES, ARTICLES HE'D HAD SPIKED.

ALL THE THINGS THAT KEPT ACTORS ON SHORT LEASHES.

THAT'S A LOT OF *MONEY* FOR A GUY WHO'S JUST MAKIN' *THREATS.*

HOW 'BOUT YOU PROVE YOU ACTUALLY *KNOW* SOMETHING...?

HOW ABOUT I PROVE IT TO THE *PAPERS* INSTEAD?

TINA SAID BRODSKY HAD GRILLED HER LIKE A *COP*... WHO ELSE WAS SHE WITH? WHEN DID SHE LEAVE THE PARTY?

SHIT. YOU GOT *NOTHIN'*... DON'T YA?

NO DOUBT HE WAS KEEPING A *RECORD* OF HIS INVESTIGATION, SO HE COULD REPORT BACK TO *MR THURSBY.*

I'M *HANGIN' UP* NOW, CHUMP.

WAIT...

I'VE GOT YOUR PROOF. VAL SOMMERS WASN'T WEARING ANY *UNDERWEAR* WHEN YOU FOUND HER, WAS SHE?

NOW GET ME MY GODDAM MONEY... *CHUMP*.

THEY JUST HAD TO *DISTRACT* HIM...

SHIT.

WHAT'S THE *HUBBUB*, CHIEF?

WE GOT WORK TO DO. LET'S GO.

GET HIM AND HIS *GOON SQUAD* OUT OF THE WAY FOR THE NIGHT...

SO *CHARLIE* COULD TRY TO GET A LOOK INSIDE HIS *OFFICE*.

THE *SHOOT* WAS ON ITS LAST DAY, AND CHARLIE FIGURED THE *WRAP PARTY* WOULD BE GOOD COVER...

HE'D FILL-UP ON *LIQUID COURAGE* AND SLIP AWAY UNSEEN.

BUT *MAYA* WAS COMPLICATING THINGS...

YOU WANT TO TAKE A WALK?

UH... PROBABLY NOT A GOOD IDEA...

NOT WITH SO MANY *EYES* WATCHING.

REALLY...?

YOU'VE HARDLY SAID A *WORD* TO ME SINCE *HALLOWEEN*, CHARLIE...

DID I MAKE A *MISTAKE*, TRUSTING YOU?

OH GOD -- WHAT WAS SHE *TALKING* ABOUT?

HE DIDN'T HAVE TIME FOR THIS.

I THOUGHT YOU'D UNDERSTAND... I THOUGHT...

BASTARD!

SAVED BY A *SUCKER PUNCH.*

TRY TO RUIN *MY MOVIE!*

KRAKK

HE'D ALMOST FORGOTTEN HOW ANGRY SCHMITT HAD BEEN WHEN HE'D REFUSED TO DO THE *REWRITES* UP IN OJAI...

BUT THE SON OF A BITCH HAD *CLEARLY* BEEN WAITING UNTIL HE DIDN'T NEED CHARLIE ANYMORE.

AND HE HAD A HELL OF A RIGHT HOOK.

NO ONE WOULD BE QUESTIONING CHARLIE'S ABSENCE NOW... THAT WAS FOR SURE.

THE HELL WAS *THAT* ABOUT, CHUCK?

FUCK IF I KNOW... *DIRECTORS* AND THEIR EGOS...

YOU SAID A MOUTHFUL *THERE.*

SO THEN... WHAT'S THE *DEAL* WITH YOU AND THE STARLET?

MAYA?

NONE OTHER.

IS SHE REPLACING OUR DEAR DEPARTED *MISS SOMMERS* IN MORE WAYS THAN *ONE*?

WHAT'S *THAT* SUPPOSED TO MEAN?

OH C'MON... EVERYONE *KNOWS* YOU HAD A THING FOR *VAL*.

THAT'S NOT... WE WERE JUST *FRIENDS*...

SURE... WHATEVER YOU *SAY*, PAL.

CHARLIE WASN'T READY TO CONFRONT EARL...

NOT UNTIL HE KNEW MORE.

BUT HERE THEY WERE, *ALONE*...

...AND HE ALREADY HAD BLOOD IN HIS MOUTH.

YOU MAKE *JOKES* ABOUT HER, LIKE NOTHING HAPPENED...

BUT YOU *KNOW* IT WASN'T LIKE THEY *SAID*.

WHAT... ARE YOU TALKING ABOUT *VAL*?

YOU *KNOW* SHE DIDN'T KILL HERSELF.

WHAT? HOW THE *HELL* WOULD I KNOW THAT?

BECAUSE YOU WERE *THERE*...

THAT NIGHT SHE DIED.

YET, EVEN AS HE SAYS IT, CHARLIE ISN'T SURE.

HE CAN PICTURE EARL WALKING THROUGH THE EMPTY PLACES IN HIS MIND... BUT IT DOESN'T FEEL LIKE A *MEMORY*.

IT FEELS LIKE A SHAPE IN THE FOG.

I'M GONNA *EXCUSE* THIS, SINCE YOU JUST GOT YOUR *HEAD* CRACKED...

BUT YOU'RE CROSSING A *LINE.*

AND YOU'VE GOT *BAD* INFORMATION.

SO YOU DIDN'T *LEAVE* WITH US?

BACK TO *VAL'S* PLACE FOR A NIGHTCAP?

CHARLIE, LISTEN TO WHAT YOU'RE *SAYING*...

WHEN HAVE YOU *EVER* KNOWN ME TO LEAVE ONE OF MY OWN PARTIES?

YOU'RE *CRACKING UP,* PAL... AND IT ISN'T PRETTY.

A MISTAKE.

SHIT!

WHY HAD HE PUSHED SO HARD?

BECAUSE IT *FELT* TRUE?

BECAUSE, OF COURSE, THE STUDIO WOULD COVER FOR SOMEONE LIKE *EARL*?

OR BECAUSE HE HATED HIMSELF FOR THE DAYS HE'D BEEN WONDERING...

COULD SOMEONE HE CALLED A FRIEND BE THAT MUCH OF A *MONSTER*?

COULD CHARLIE BE THAT BLINDED BY FAME AND GLAMOUR?

HIS HANDS SHAKE AS HE FINISHES PUTTING ON HIS DISGUISE.

IT HAD BEEN A MISTAKE, TALKING TO EARL...

AND NOW HE WAS RUNNING LATE TO MAKE ANOTHER ONE.

NIGHT, MORTY...

NIGHT.

THE SECURITY OFFICES WERE ALL EMPTY.

BRODSKY WAS SO COCKY HE HADN'T EVEN LOCKED HIS DOOR.

IT WAS JUST A MATTER OF *FINDING* SOMETHING NOW...

AND GETTING OUT BEFORE THEY CAME BACK.

BUT AFTER TWENTY MINUTES OF FUTILE SEARCHING, HIS NERVES GET TO HIM AGAIN...

SHIT.

THIS IS A FOOL'S ERRAND.

WHAT WAS HE THINKING?

THAT BRODSKY WOULD JUST LEAVE HIM A TRAIL OF BREADCRUMBS?

WHAT THE FUCK...?

MILLER, DRAKE

DRAKE MILLER'S FILE. IT'S THIN.

ONLY TWO THINGS IN IT. TWO *PHOTOGRAPHS*.

AND THE FIRST ONE ANSWERS CHARLIE'S NAGGING QUESTION ABOUT EARL RATH.

THERE THEY ALL WERE, LEAVING THE PARTY THAT NIGHT... CHARLIE, HIS BACK TO THE CAMERA... THEN VAL, DRAKE MILLER, TINA...

AND TYLER GRAVES. *NOT* EARL.

TINA HAD SAID "YOUR *MOVIE STAR* FRIEND."

SHIT.

HE'S CURSING HIMSELF FOR HIS STUPIDITY...

... WHEN THE *NEXT* PICTURE TAKES HIS BREATH AWAY.

IT'S NOTHING SALACIOUS, LIKE THE PHOTOS GIL HAD STOLEN...

JUST A HEADSHOT OF A CHILD ACTRESS.

BUT HE KNOWS HER FACE...

AND THE NAME ON THE BACK.

A FORGOTTEN NAME.

Jenny Summ

JENNY SUMMERS WAS VAL'S *REAL* NAME...

SHE USED IT BACK IN THE *KRAZY KIDS* DAYS, WHEN SHE WAS NOBODY.

SO THERE'S A PICTURE OF A KID IN A FILE. SO *WHAT?*

IT'S WEIRD, *THAT'S* WHAT.

BRODSKY'S GETTING RID OF OLD MAN KAMP'S SICK STASH OF *KIDDIE* PICS...

AND NOW THIS GUY, WHO WAS *THERE* WHEN VAL *DIED*...

ALL THAT'S IN HIS FILE IS A PHOTO OF HER FROM *TWENTY YEARS* AGO?

DON'T *TELL ME* THERE'S NOT A *CONNECTION* HERE...

JESUS, CHARLIE... WHEN YOU STEP IN IT...

YOU JUST *LEAP* IN WITH *BOTH FEET*, DON'T YOU?

I SHOULD'VE KNOWN YOU WERE UP TO *NO GOOD* WHEN YOU STARTED ASKING QUESTIONS ABOUT *DRAKE MILLER*...

WHO YOU SAID YOU'D NEVER *HEARD* OF.

BECAUSE I WAS TRYING TO *PROTECT* YOU.

THAT MAN'S *NOTHING* BUT BAD NEWS.

EARL SAID THERE WAS A *PRODUCER* ON THE LOT THAT WAS AN *FBI PLANT*...

IS IT *DRAKE MILLER?*

WHY DO YOU *THINK* THAT?

JUST THE WAY HE *TALKED* TO ME...

LIKE THERE WAS A *THREAT* UNDER EVERYTHING.

I'M SURE YOU UNDERSTAND THE *DELICATE NATURE* OF THIS SITUATION, DOROTHY...

YOU MIGHT SURVIVE THE SCANDAL... YOU'RE A *NOBODY*, AFTER ALL...

BUT YOUR... *FRIEND?*

WELL, MRS MOONEY'S A *STAR*, ISN'T SHE?

AND *MARRIED*, TO BOOT.

WHAT DO YOU WANT?

SO I'M *RIGHT?* HE WORKS FOR THE *FEDS?*

WHAT'S HE DOING, HUNTING *COMMIES?*

YES... AND YOU *KNOW* HOW THEY OPERATE...

FIND SOMEONE'S DIRTIEST SECRET AND USE IT *AGAINST* THEM.

BUT IT'S NOT LIKE WE'VE NEVER HEARD OF *BLACKMAIL* IN THE MOVIE BUSINESS...

NO *SURPRISE* EVERYONE THINKS HE'S A REAL PRODUCER.

SO, THAT PICTURE OF VAL AS A *KID.* WHO WOULD THAT BE A *THREAT* TO --

CHARLIE -- *STOP.*

DON'T YOU *GET IT?* YOU CAN'T MESS AROUND WITH THESE PEOPLE...

NOT THE STUDIO BOSSES, AND *CERTAINLY* NOT THE *FBI.*

I'M TRYING TO DO THE RIGHT THING, DOT.

WHY? THE RIGHT THING ISN'T GOING TO BRING *VAL* BACK.

LISTEN -- YOU NEED TO LET THIS *GO,* CHARLIE.

YOU NEED TO GO FIND *EARL* AND CONVINCE HIM THAT YOU WERE JUST MAKING A STUPID *DRUNKEN* JOKE...

THAT YOU DON'T KNOW *ANYTHING* ABOUT VAL'S DEATH...

THEN YOU NEED TO GO HOME AND TELL *GIL* THAT THIS LITTLE FANTASY IS *OVER.*

I CAN'T DO THAT.

WHY NOT? BECAUSE YOU'RE SUDDENLY GOING TO TURN INTO *SHERLOCK HOLMES* OR *SAM SPADE?*

WAKE UP...

THERE ARE NO *GOOD GUYS* IN REAL LIFE, CHARLIE.

PLEASE TAKE MY ADVICE AND FORGET ABOUT ALL OF THIS...

BUT DOTTIE KNOWS THAT HE WON'T...

SHE CAN SEE IT IN HIS EYES, BEFORE SHE TURNS AWAY.

BUT WHAT SHE DOESN'T KNOW, WHAT SHE CAN'T KNOW...

IS THAT EVEN IF HE WANTED TO, CHARLIE *COULDN'T* QUIT NOW.

SOMETHING SHE SAID ABOUT THE FBI'S *METHODS* STRUCK A CHORD IN HIS *MEMORY*...

AND NOW HE THINKS HE KNOWS HOW LITTLE *JENNY SUMMERS* CONNECTS TOGETHER EVERYTHING THAT'S HAPPENED.

LESS THAN AN HOUR LATER, CHARLIE AND GIL ARE ON THE ROAD TO *OJAI*...

HEADING STRAIGHT FOR OLD MAN KAMP.

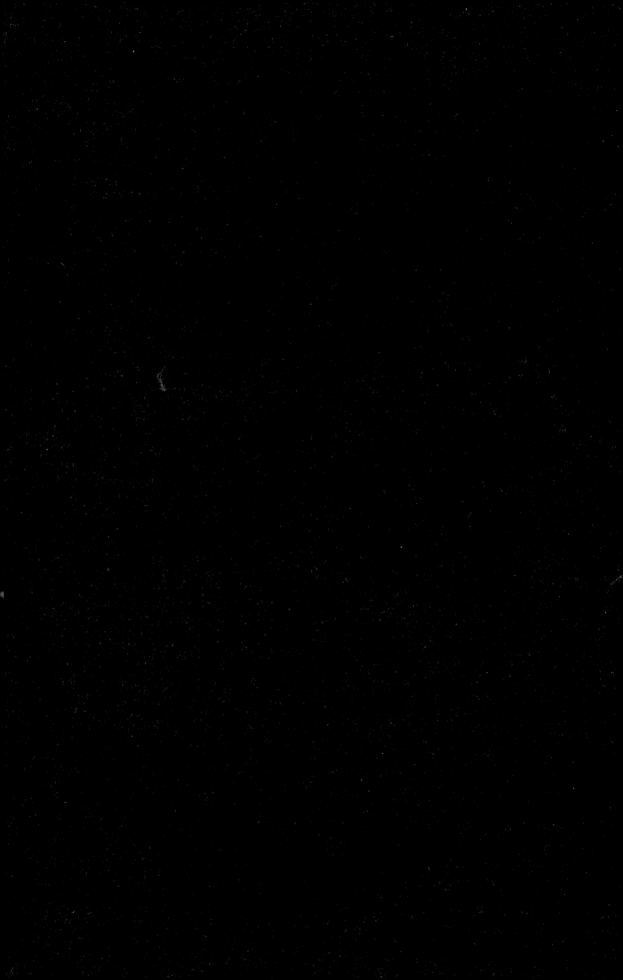

Anyone Else But Me

It was about a week before Earl's party...

Remember? That day we shut down production because Val was a *no-show*?

Dottie tracked her down, somehow, and sent *me* to go fetch her back...

SOUNDS LIKE SHE NEEDS A FRIEND AND SHE *LIKES* YOU, CHARLIE...

GOD ONLY KNOWS *WHY*.

PROBABLY MY DASHING *GOOD LOOKS*...

WELL, IT *CAN'T* BE YOUR SENSE OF HUMOR.

I had to look the address up on the map...

It was this little spot north of *Malibu*, lots of windy roads to get there.

Not much traffic.

I could see why *this* would be her escape.

For a second or two, I wanted to join her on it.

HELLO...?

VAL...?

But then I saw her, the state she was in, and all those kind of thoughts...

The way men always think...

They just disappeared.

OKAY... LET'S GET YOU UP...

OH... CHARLIE...

I just wanted to take care of her, make sure she was okay.

It took two cups of coffee before she even tried to explain what happened...

Why she'd run off and gotten plastered to the point of a near-breakdown.

She was so fragile as she spoke, I kept expecting her to fall apart again... But she didn't.

She just talked about how funny it was that your past never really went away.

Even in Hollywood, for all the effort they put into burying everyone's past... It was still there, waiting.

Waiting to find you at the right moment, and turn you back into a scared little kid again.

I had nothing to say to that, because I understood exactly what she meant...

And hearing her say it had sent me straight down my own rabbit hole.

Thinking about the things in my past that didn't seem to want to stay there.

I was so caught up, I almost didn't notice when she started telling me her story...

Or, as much of it as she could put into words, at least.

There was the child actress, with the stage mother who'd gotten pregnant on the set of a *Fairbanks* picture.

Mom had missed her shot at stardom, so the daughter would have to do whatever it took.

Anything to gain favor with the producers.

She didn't say what "anything" consisted of, but the way she said the word, you just knew.

...BUT IT DIDN'T END *BADLY*, FUNNY ENOUGH. YOU'D THINK IT WOULD *HAVE* TO...

BUT THERE WAS A *KIND* MAN WHO SAVED ME FROM THAT LIFE.

HE HELPED ME *STOP* BEING JENNY.

HE PROTECTED ME.

BUT EVEN *KINDNESS* CAN BE EXPLOITED, CAN'T IT? BY PEOPLE LOOKING FOR DIRT.

THE PAST IS A *KNIFE*, CHARLIE...

THAT'S WHAT I THINK.

I probably *was* in love with her, right at that moment. But not in that "want to sweep her off her feet" way.

No, in the way where you just feel it inside, wherever your soul must be.

That's probably why I told her so much.

She had showed herself to me, and now it was my turn.

All my pathetic secrets... What happened in Germany...

How I couldn't write anymore...

How I was *fronting* for Gil so we could both survive...

Everything.

And afterwards, there was nothing but understanding.

We slept in our clothes, just holding each other...

Like little kids trying to sleep through a thunderstorm.

But in the middle of the night, I woke up filled with this kind of... dread.

I went out to listen to the waves, hoping it would help...

But instead, I thought about swimming into them, just swimming away from everything.

Val had given me a few hours of peace, of remembering what it felt like to really be *alive*...

Instead of whatever it was I'd *been* since I came home.

But the sun was going to rise soon, and we'd go back to real life... Back to our roles.

And god damn, I wished I could stop that from happening.

...THEN SHE SAID, "THE PAST IS A *KNIFE*."

AND SEE, I DIDN'T KNOW WHAT SHE WAS TALKING ABOUT, EXACTLY...

BUT *NOW* I THINK I DO.

DOTTIE SAYS THIS FAKE *PRODUCER* -- THIS DRAKE MILLER -- HAS BEEN DIGGING UP EVERYONE'S DIRTIEST SECRETS, USING THEM AS *LEVERAGE*...

IT ALL JUST *FITS*... DOESN'T IT?

WHAT *YOU* FOUND... THOSE PICTURES...

VAL ACTING SO *DISTRAUGHT* THAT DAY...

THAT *FBI* SON OF A BITCH WAS *LEANING* ON HER.

HE HAD TO BE.

I THINK MAYBE *SOMEHOW* DRAKE MILLER GOT HIS HANDS ON SOME OF KAMP'S *OLD PICTURES*... JUST LIKE WE DID...

MAYBE *THAT'S* WHY HE'S ABLE TO OPERATE RIGHT THERE ON THE LOT.

HE'S *GOT* SOMETHING ON THE BOSSES.

WAIT... WAS *MILLER* BLACKMAILING THE STUDIO OR *VAL?*

WHY NOT *BOTH?*

IF HE'S GOT *PROOF* OF OLD MAN KAMP'S *PRIVATE PARTIES*...

WHAT THOSE BASTARDS *DID* TO VAL AND THOSE OTHER KIDS...

WHY WOULDN'T HE USE IT AGAINST *EVERYONE* HE CAN?

EVEN THE VICTIM.

SO VAL SOMMERS GOT CAUGHT IN THE *CROSSFIRE* BETWEEN *VICTORY STREET* AND THE FEDS?

I THINK SO, YEAH... *MAYBE.*

SHE CONNECTS TO EVERYTHING... FROM WAY BACK WHEN, RIGHT UP TO NOW.

MILLER *MUST'VE* FOUND SOMETHING WITH HER *IN* IT...

...BACK WHEN SHE WAS STILL JUST *LITTLE JENNY.*

IT *DOES* FEEL LIKE THE FBI'S STYLE...

TURNING A BLIND EYE TO *REAL EVIL* SO THEY CAN ROOT OUT *COMMIES.*

BUT I WOULDN'T NECESSARILY SAY YOU'VE *CRACKED* THE CASE, PAL.

YOU'VE GOT THREE THEORIES, AND THEY'RE ALL FULL OF *MAYBES*.

WHENEVER WE WRITE DETECTIVE FLICKS, *MAYBES* USUALLY MEAN HOLES IN THE PLOT.

ONE OF THEM WAS *YOUR* THEORY, I'M JUST *AGREEING* WITH YOU...

DRAKE MILLER, OLD MAN KAMP, VAL'S MURDER...

IT'S ALL TIED-UP *TOGETHER*, SOMEHOW.

I GUESS THE *SOMEHOW* DOESN'T MATTER, REALLY.

WE'RE GONNA FIND *SOMETHING* UP THERE... ONE WAY OR THE OTHER...

THEY'D STOPPED ON THE ROAD TO OLD MAN KAMP'S *RANCH* TO MAKE A RUDIMENTARY PLAN...

SO THEY WOULDN'T JUST BE RUSHING IN WITHOUT THINKING IT OVER FIRST.

BUT THEIR *PLAN* WASN'T MUCH TO SPEAK OF.

OLD MAN KAMP WAS SENILE AND DELUSIONAL.

SO THEY WERE GOING TO WAKE HIM JUST AFTER MIDNIGHT, GET HIM EVEN MORE DISORIENTED THAN USUAL.

THEY'LL SAY THEY'RE FROM THE STUDIO, SENT BY *THURSBY* TO TAKE HIM WHORING.

SNEAK HIM OUT TO THE CAR, GET A FEW *DRINKS* IN HIM....

THE OLD MAN WILL COUGH UP WHATEVER THEY WANT TO KNOW.

ASSUMING HE'S LUCID.

ASSUMING HE FOLLOWS THEIR SCRIPT.

WE SHOULD SEE IF HE'S GOT ANYTHING TO *RECORD* ON...

MAYBE WE CAN GET HIM ON A *REEL-TO-REEL* OR SOMETHING?

YEAH, MAYBE... BUT *YOU'RE* CARRYING IT IF WE FIND ONE.

THOSE FUCKERS ARE *HEAVY.*

I'M NOT HAULING IT ALL THE WAY BACK HERE.

CHARLIE HAD BEEN TO THE RANCH SEVERAL TIMES THE PAST FEW MONTHS, AND KNEW THE PLACE WAS OPERATING WITH A SKELETON CREW.

KAMP WAS JUST A *FIGUREHEAD* NOW. THE STUDIO TOOK CARE OF HIM, BUT THEY KEPT THEIR COSTS LOW.

THE ONLY STAFF THIS LATE WOULD BE THE MAID, MAYBE A NURSE... AND A SECURITY GUARD AT THE *GATE...*

CREEZUS...

BUT THEY WERE BYPASSING THAT.

HEY... HOW WE GONNA GET THE OLD MAN OVER THAT *FENCE*?

I DON'T KNOW. WE'LL FIGURE IT OUT.

SHIT.

HOW *WERE* THEY GOING TO GET KAMP OVER THAT FENCE?

AND WHAT IF THE OLD MAN *DIDN'T* FOLLOW THEIR SCRIPT?

WHAT IF HE JUST STARTED SCREAMING HIS –

GET DOWN -- *CAR*.

SHIT.

SHIT SHIT SHIT SHIT SHIT.

DAMMIT... THAT WAS CLOSE... WE SHOULD GET *OUT* OF HERE.

WHAT? NOT ON YOUR *LIFE*, PAL.

SOMEONE WAS JUST *HERE*, GIL.

THAT COULD'VE BEEN ANYONE. MAYBE THE GODDAM *BUTLER* STAYED LATE?

WE'RE NOT TURNING BACK.

I'M NOT, AT LEAST.

JESUS. IS THAT *MY* GUN?

YEAH... I CAME PREPARED.

YOU'RE GONNA PULL A *GUN* ON AN OLD MAN?

IF THAT'S WHAT I *HAVE* TO DO.

NOW, C'MON...

FUCKIN' GIL.

HE'D SPENT HALF AN HOUR POKING HOLES IN CHARLIE'S STORY, YET HERE HE WAS... JUST CHARGING AHEAD.

HE DIDN'T REALLY CARE ABOUT VAL...

ABOUT FINDING OUT WHO KILLED HER OR WHY...

GIL WAS AFTER SOMETHING BIGGER.

A SAILOR AT WAR WITH THE WIND AND THE SEA.

GIL, HEY... THIS IS --

SHHHHH -- !

NO. OF COURSE HE WON'T LISTEN.

THEY'RE GOING TO GET *CAUGHT*, CHARLIE THINKS.

THEY'RE GOING TO GET CAUGHT AND THEY'RE NOT GOING TO FIND OUT *ANYTHING* ABOUT VAL OR DRAKE MILLER...

DRAKE MILLER... WITH THAT SMUG PRICK SMILE THAT'S BEEN NAGGING AT HIM...

PRODUCE! ON THE LO1 *VICTORY STREET*, MEAN.

THAT SMILE... THAT STUPID FUCKING SMILE...

Y'KNOW, I'M A BIG FAN.

THAT'S WHAT *DOES* IT, FINALLY...

"AT THE END" IS STILL ONE OF MY FAVORITE PICTURES.

KICKS OPEN ANOTHER ONE OF CHARLIE'S *BLACKOUT* DOORS.

OH, THANKS...

SHAME YOU HAD TO GO UP AGAINST *"CITIZEN KANE"* AT THE OSCARS...

OTHERWISE YOU'D HAVE HAD IT IN THE BAG.

THAT WAS A LONG TIME AGO.

TRUE... IT WAS.

STILL, I'VE KEPT AN *EYE* ON YOU, CHARLIE...

YOUR WORK, I MEAN.

AND YOUR RECENT STUFF, IT'S JUST *NOT* THE SAME.

SOMETIMES IT DOESN'T EVEN SOUND LIKE *YOUR WRITING* AT ALL.

HEY FELLAS, HOW ARE THOSE DRINKS COMING?

SORRY, JUST GETTING TO KNOW YOUR FRIEND *CHARLIE* HERE...

THERE'S A LOOK IN VAL'S EYE AS SHE LEADS DRAKE MILLER AWAY... UNEASY, WORRIED.

HE REMEMBERS THAT NOW.

AND HER ANGRY HUSHED TONES IN THE HALLWAY.

TOLD YOU HIM ALONE

BUT – WAIT... *THAT* CONVERSATION...

THAT WASN'T AT *VAL'S* PLACE... WAS IT?

SHIT.

THIS WAS OLD MAN KAMP'S *SCREENING ROOM*...

I WAS AT A *PARTY* HERE ONE TIME... THOSE SHELVES WERE FULL OF FILM CANS...

THEY GOT RID OF EVERYTHING.

ALMOST EVERYTHING...

THEY LEFT "*THE KRAZY KIDS CHRISTMAS CAROL.*"

SHIT.

HIS MAID AND NURSE AREN'T HERE, EITHER...

BOTH THEIR ROOMS WERE EMPTY.

THIS WHOLE GODDAM HOUSE IS *EMPTY*, CHARLIE.

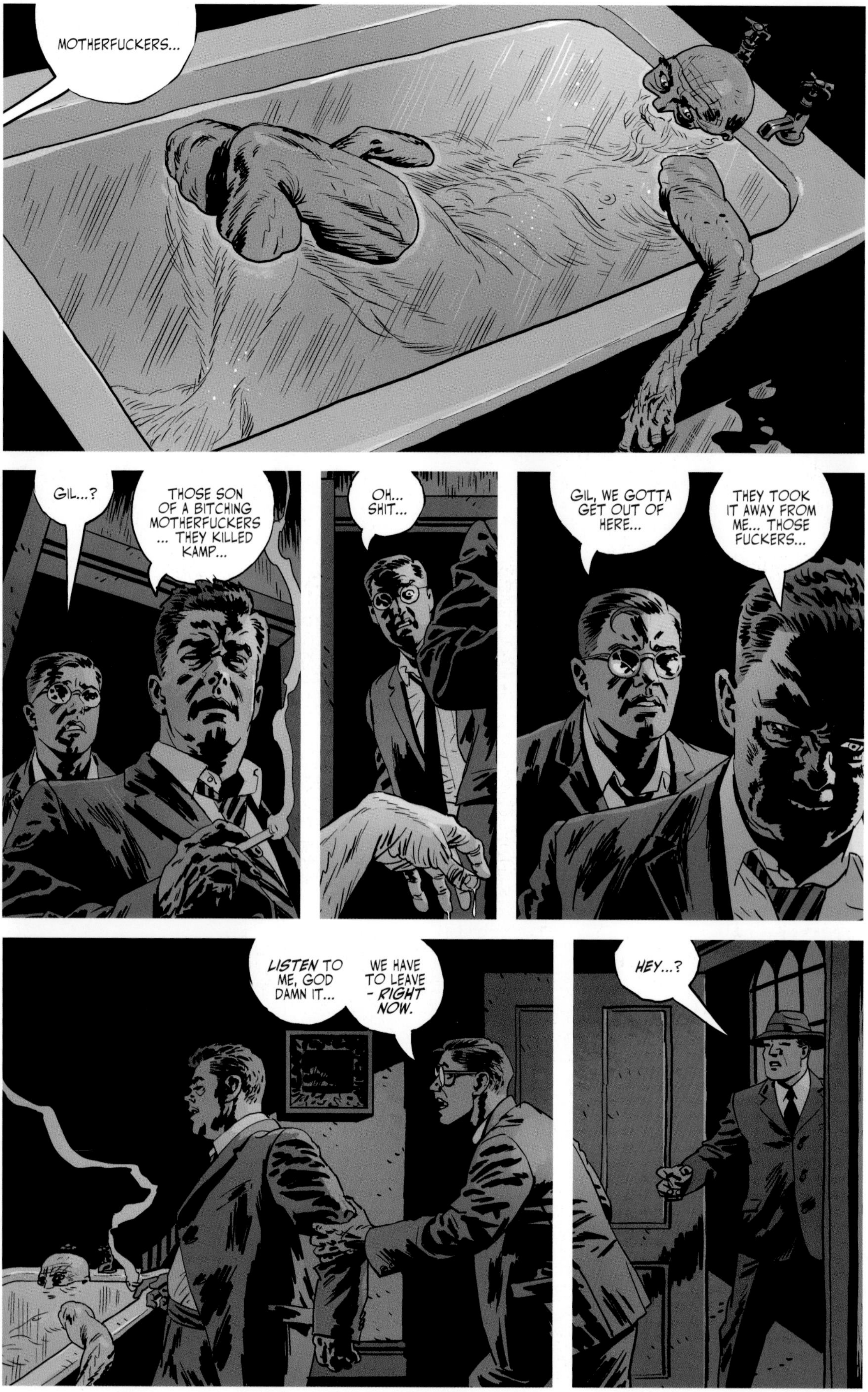
MOTHERFUCKERS...
GIL...?
THOSE SON OF A BITCHING MOTHERFUCKERS ... THEY KILLED KAMP...
OH... SHIT...
GIL, WE GOTTA GET OUT OF HERE...
THEY TOOK IT AWAY FROM ME... THOSE FUCKERS...
LISTEN TO ME, GOD DAMN IT...
WE HAVE TO LEAVE - RIGHT NOW.
HEY...?

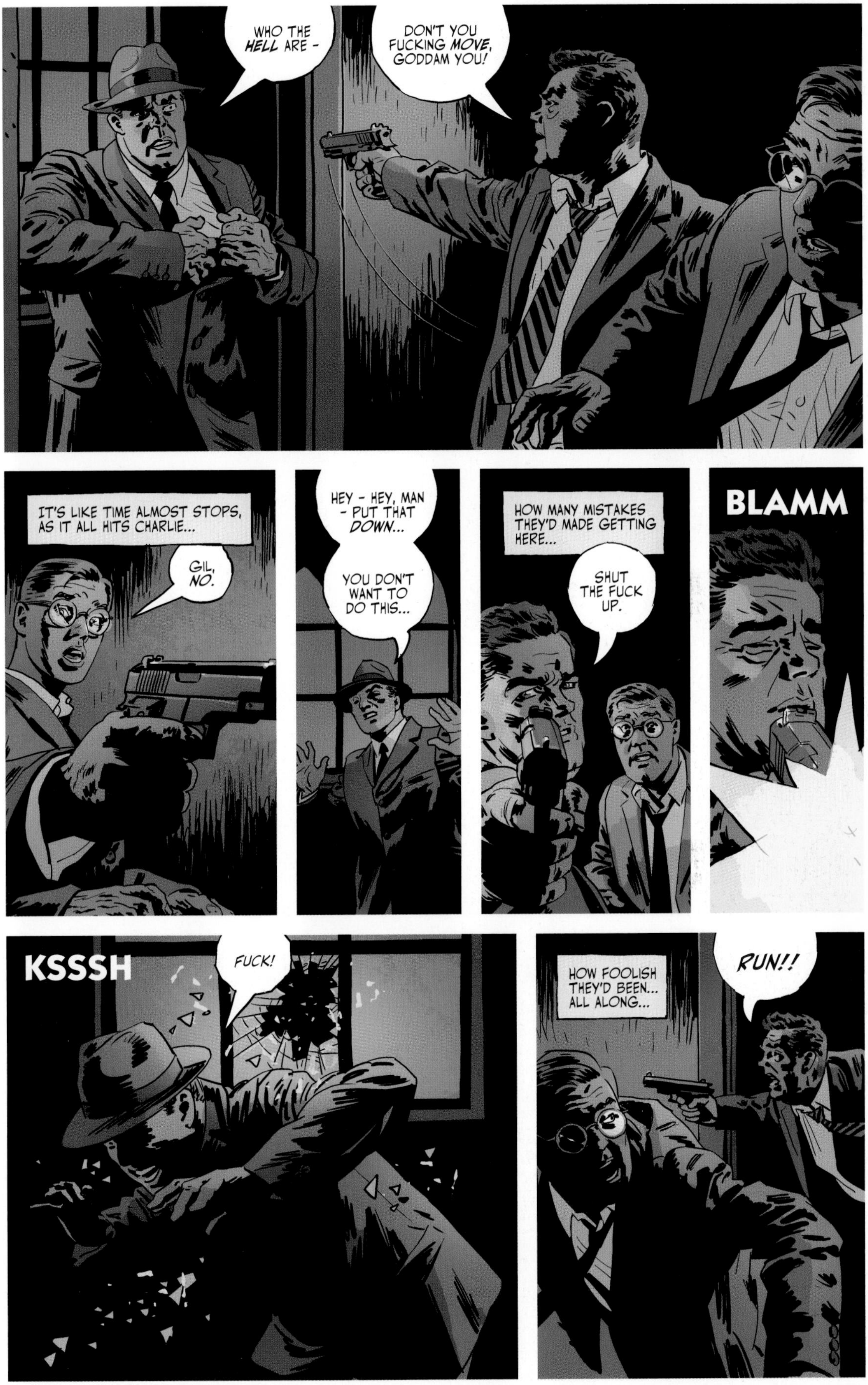
WHO THE *HELL* ARE -
DON'T YOU FUCKING *MOVE*, GODDAM YOU!
IT'S LIKE TIME ALMOST STOPS, AS IT ALL HITS CHARLIE...
GIL, *NO*.
HEY - HEY, MAN - PUT THAT *DOWN*...
YOU DON'T WANT TO DO THIS...
HOW MANY MISTAKES THEY'D MADE GETTING HERE...
SHUT THE FUCK UP.
BLAMM
KSSSH
FUCK!
HOW FOOLISH THEY'D BEEN... ALL ALONG...
RUN!!

THEY HAD EXPECTED TO BE... WHAT?

DETECTIVES? HEROES?

BLAMM BLAM BLAM

JESUS!

WHAT A SHAM.

THEY WERE TWO BROKEN-DOWN WRITERS...

RUNNING ON *DESPERATION* AND BOOZE...

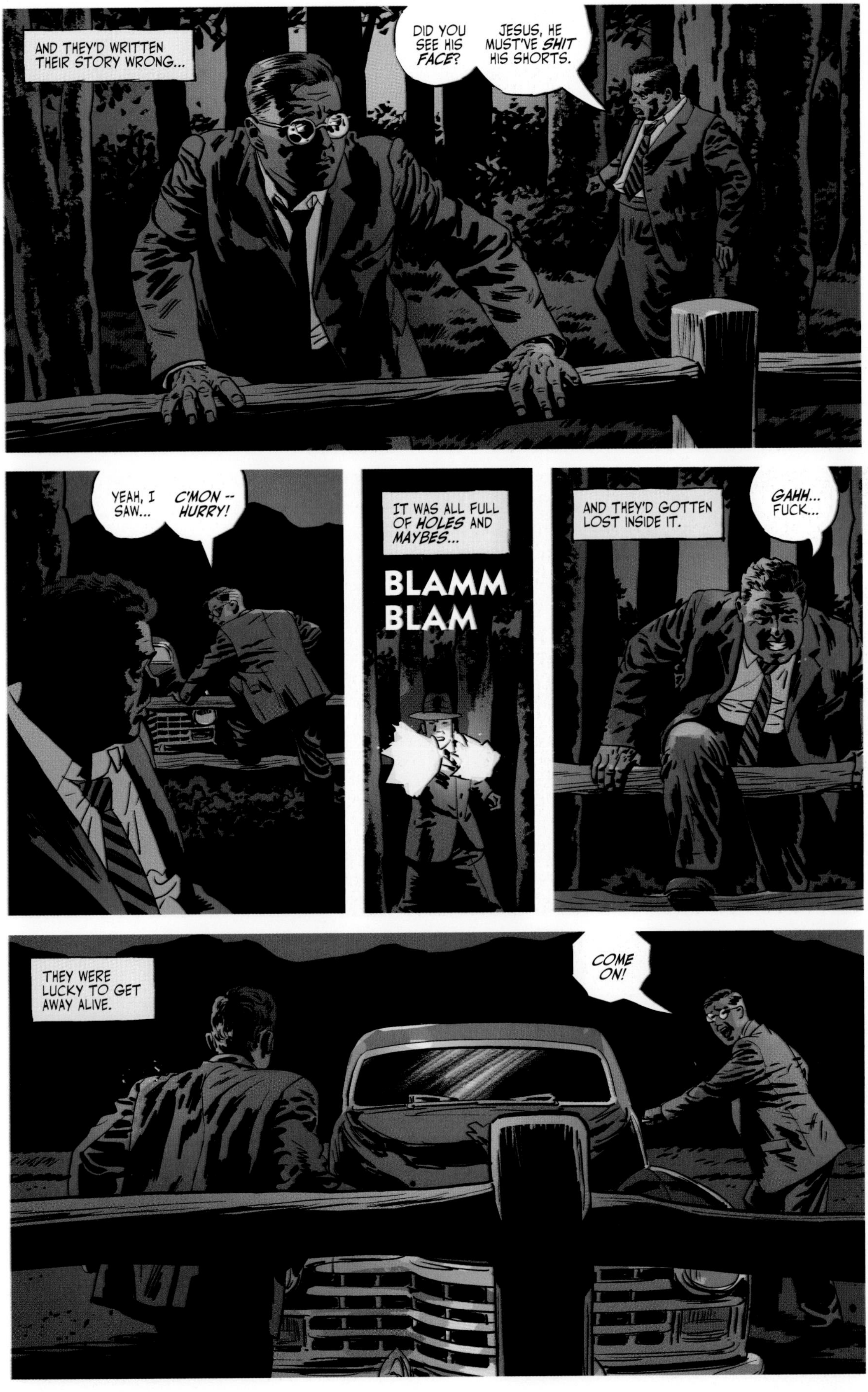
AND THEY'D WRITTEN THEIR STORY WRONG...
DID YOU SEE HIS FACE?
JESUS, HE MUST'VE SHIT HIS SHORTS.
YEAH, I SAW...
C'MON -- HURRY!
IT WAS ALL FULL OF HOLES AND MAYBES...
BLAMM BLAM
AND THEY'D GOTTEN LOST INSIDE IT.
GAHH... FUCK...
THEY WERE LUCKY TO GET AWAY ALIVE.
COME ON!

BUT NOW, *WHAT*...? THEY'D HAVE TO LEAVE TOWN FOR A WHILE...

KEEP YOUR *HEAD* DOWN... HE'S STILL BACK THERE...

OR... *FOREVER*?

WAS THIS IT?

CHARLIE'S MIND RACES...

DAMMIT... WE'RE IN *BIG TROUBLE* HERE, PAL...

LIKE HE ALMOST CAN'T BELIEVE HOW BADLY THEY'VE SCREWED UP...

CHRIST. THEY WERE LUCKY TO GET AWAY ALIVE.

GIL...?

OH... OH SHIT...

Tomorrow, When the World is Free

JUST BEFORE CHARLIE WAKES UP...

SPLINTERS OF MEMORY...

...ASSAULT HIS MIND.

LIKE REALITY CAN'T WAIT TO COLLAPSE IN ON HIM.

...FUCK...

??

MAYA? WHERE THE HELL WAS HE?

CHAVEZ RAVINE... THE *MEXICAN* PART OF TOWN. HE KNEW THIS PLACE.

THERE WAS A WHOREHOUSE HERE THAT GIL ENDED UP AT SOMETIMES...

SHIT -- GIL.

WHERE WAS HIS CAR?

OH, THANK GOD...

CHARLIE...?

ARE YOU LEAVING? WERE YOU NOT GOING TO WAKE ME?

NO, I JUST...

HOW DID WE *GET* HERE?

YOU *CALLED ME* IN THE MIDDLE OF THE NIGHT...

SAID YOU NEEDED SOMEPLACE TO *HIDE OUT.*

YOU SCARED THE *HELL* OUT OF ME, CHARLIE... DON'T YOU REMEMBER?

DOES HE? IT SOUNDS RIGHT.

...JUS'... JUS' LISSEN, DAMMIT...

BUT ALL HE CAN *REALLY* REMEMBER FROM LAST NIGHT ARE GIL'S DEAD EYES.

SO, WHY HIDE *HERE*, THOUGH?

THIS IS MY *MOTHER'S* HOUSE.

NO ONE WILL FIND US HERE.

BUT WHAT ON EARTH ARE YOU --

SHIT, THERE'S BLOOD ON HIS CLOTHES.

I NEED A CLEAN SHIRT...

I'LL GET YOU ONE OF MY FATHER'S... SHE'S NEVER THROWN OUT HIS THINGS...

BUT YOU HAVE TO TELL ME WHAT *HAPPENED*.

I CAN'T HELP YOU IF I DON'T KNOW HOW BAD IT IS.

HOW BAD... CHRIST, ALL HE'S GOT IS BAD.

A DEAD BEST FRIEND IN HIS CAR...

AND WHO KNOWS HOW LONG UNTIL BRODSKY AND HIS BOYS TRACK HIM DOWN?

NOT MUCH TIME AT ALL. BARELY ENOUGH.

WAIT... YOUR MOTHER?

YOU'RE *MEXICAN*?

I THOUGHT YOU *KNEW*, AFTER THE OTHER NIGHT WITH ARMANDO...

NO... I MEAN, IT DOESN'T *MATTER*, I JUST...

WHAT?

I NEED TO BORROW YOUR CAR.

JESUS, CHARLIE... DO YOU EVEN SEE ME *AT ALL*?

AND THE TRUTH WAS, SOME PART OF HIM *DID*... SOME PART OF HIM SAW THE *RISK* MAYA HAD TAKEN FOR HIM...

SAW THAT SHE'D *REVEALED* HERSELF.

BUT THE *OTHER* PARTS OF CHARLIE, THEY WERE ONLY SEEING *GHOSTS* NOW...

AND NO SAD EYES WOULD DISTRACT HIM FROM ALL THE *DEATH* IN HIS HEAD.

THE STUDIO HAD COVERED-UP EVERYTHING... THEY'D EVEN KILLED OLD MAN KAMP TO KEEP THE LID ON HIS SICK PERVERSIONS.

THEY'D ALL GOTTEN AWAY WITH IT... BUT *SOMEONE* HAD TO PAY.

FOR GIL... FOR VALERIA SOMMERS...

SOMEONE *HAD* TO PAY.

AND SO HE PICKED *DRAKE MILLER.*

BECAUSE HE WAS *THERE* THE NIGHT VAL DIED...

BECAUSE THAT SMUG PRICK SMILE SAID HE THOUGHT HE WAS *UNTOUCHABLE*...

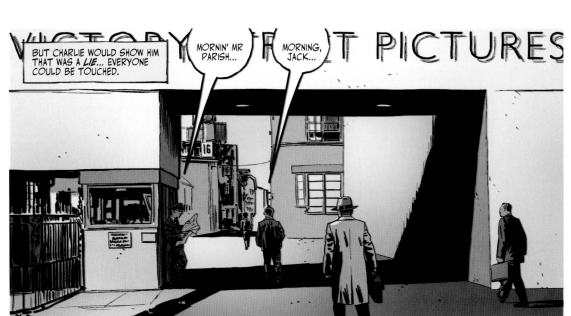

BUT CHARLIE WOULD SHOW HIM THAT WAS A *LIE*... EVERYONE COULD BE TOUCHED.

MORNIN' MR PARISH...

MORNING, JACK...

THAT WAS WHAT THE WORLD DID.

CHARLIE WOULD SHOW HIM...

AND -

??

Drak.
Miller

NO.

CAN I *HELP YOU*, BUDDY?

Drak.
Miller

I WAS... UH... I WAS LOOKING FOR DRAKE MILLER...

HEAR HE TOOK ANOTHER JOB SOMEWHERE...

WHAT WERE YOU LOOKING FOR *HIM* FOR?

OH... UM... HE JUST...

WE WERE SUPPOSED TO TALK... ABOUT WORK...

MAYBE I BETTER GET YOUR NAME.

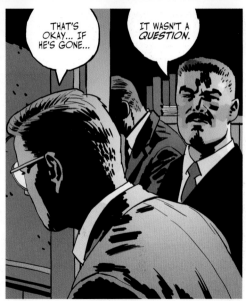

THAT'S OKAY... IF HE'S GONE...

IT WASN'T A *QUESTION*.

YOUR NAME. NOW.

EASE OFF, CHESTER...

I KNOW THIS GUY.

LONG TIME NO SEE, PARISH...

THEY WEREN'T BRODSKY'S MEN, THEY WERE *FBI*.

AND THIS ONE WAS ANOTHER FACE CHARLIE HAD TRIED TO *FORGET*...

JUST SIGN AT THE BOTTOM THERE, LIKE A CONTRACT...

THE AGENT HE'D GIVEN GIL'S NAME TO LAST YEAR.

WHO'D MADE HIM REALIZE THAT EVEN *PHONY* BETRAYAL...

THAT'S IT, GOOD BOY.

...STILL FELT LIKE *BETRAYAL*.

I DON'T KNOW WHAT HAPPENED WITH MILLER... BUT THE *BOSSES* WANTED HIM *BACK EAST* ALL OF A SUDDEN.

GUESS THERE'S COMMIES ON *BROADWAY*, TOO...

YEAH, I GUESS SO...

BUT LISTEN, CHARLIE, WE'VE BEEN HEARING SOME *THINGS* ABOUT YOU...

THINGS THAT HAVE GOT US A BIT *CONCERNED*, ACTUALLY.

I DON'T KNOW WHAT YOU MEAN.

TELL YOU WHAT... STOP BY MY *OFFICE* TOMORROW AND WE'LL GET TO THE BOTTOM OF THE WHOLE THING...

HOW'S THAT SOUND?

HE FELT SEASICK.

OF COURSE THE FBI WOULD MAKE DRAKE MILLER DISAPPEAR...

OF COURSE CHARLIE WOULDN'T GET ANYTHING... NOT EVEN REVENGE...

AS A STAND-IN FOR JUSTICE.

AND IN THAT MOMENT, HE SAW *WHY* THINGS ALWAYS WENT WRONG FOR HIM NOW...

HE UNDERSTOOD HIS PROBLEM.

IT WAS THAT HE'D LOST THE ABILITY TO IMAGINE WHAT HAPPENED NEXT.

CHARLIE COULD ONLY THINK AS FAR AS THE NEXT DRINK ANYMORE...

COULD ONLY EXIST ON THE EDGE OF OBLIVION.

NOW THE FBI HAD TAKEN AWAY HIS LAST MOVE... AND HE WAS CAST ADRIFT.

WHAT HAPPENED NEXT?

HE HADN'T THOUGHT BEYOND KILLING DRAKE MILLER.

WHAT THE HELL WAS HE GOING TO DO NOW?

HE COULD STILL RUN... BUT THE PROBLEM WAS GIL.

HE COULDN'T JUST DUMP HIM BY THE SIDE OF THE ROAD AND DRIVE AWAY.

HE COULDN'T DO THAT TO *MELBA*.

NO, SHE DESERVED THE TRUTH... AND AFTER THAT...

WHAT CAME NEXT?

HE KNEW MELBA. SHE'D GO TO THE *POLICE*...

AND THE COPS WOULD SWEEP IT ALL UNDER THE RUG.

SO THEN SHE'D GO TO THE *PRESS*, INSTEAD...

BUT THE *STUDIO* WOULD BE READY WITH THEIR OWN BAD NEWS...

CHARLIE WOULD BE EXPOSED AS A *FRAUD*, FRONTING FOR A *BLACKLISTED* COMMIE.

GIL WOULD BE *BLAMED* FOR EVERYTHING, MAYBE EVEN OLD MAN KAMP'S MURDER... MAYBE EVEN VALERIA SOMMERS'.

MELBA'S LIFE, HER CHILDREN'S LIVES, WOULD BE RUINED.

JESUS CHRIST... THERE *HAD* TO BE ANOTHER WAY...

SOMETHING *ELSE* THAT COULD HAPPEN NEXT...

SOMETHING —

OH, GOOD, YOU'RE *BACK*...

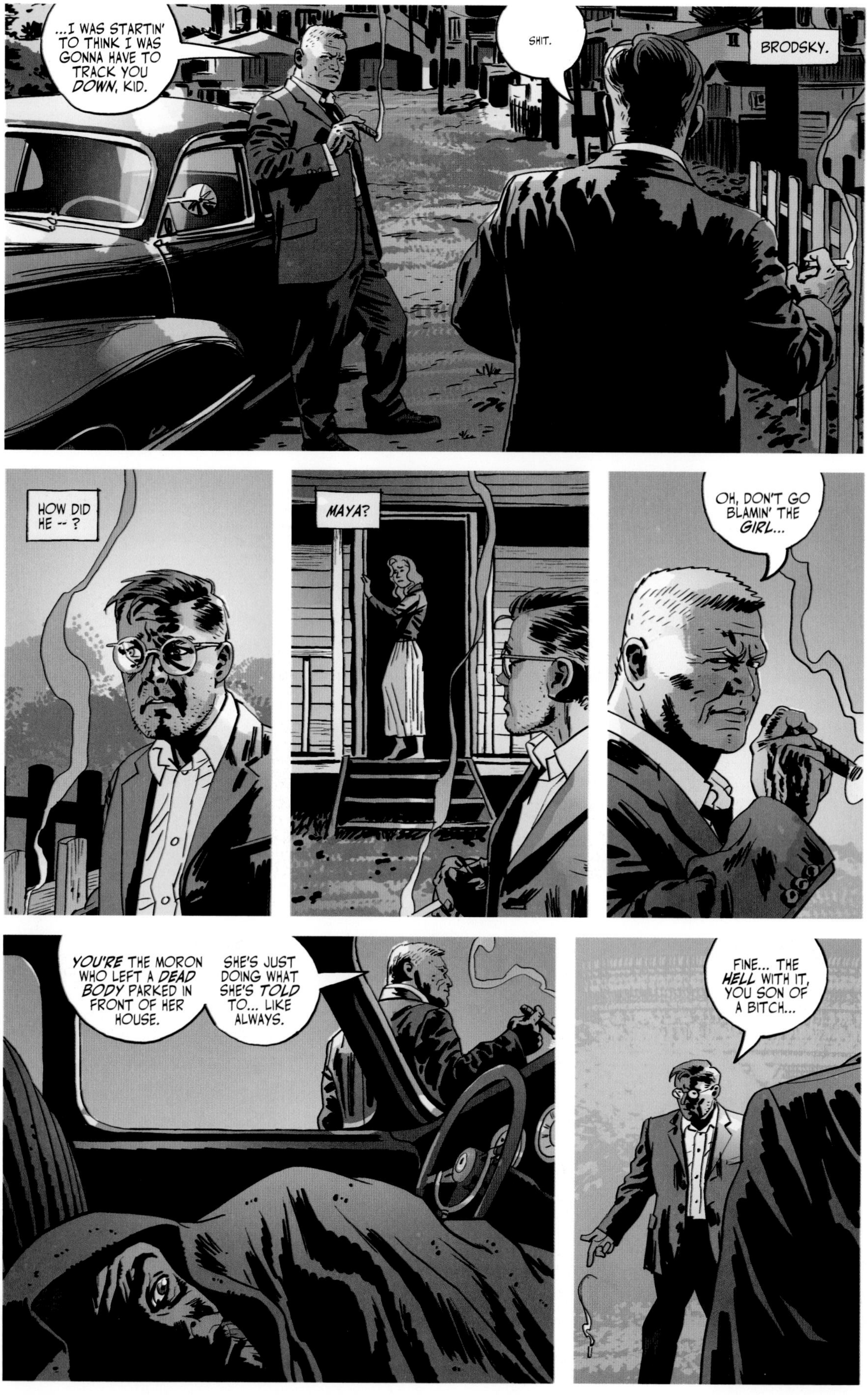
...I WAS STARTIN' TO THINK I WAS GONNA HAVE TO TRACK YOU DOWN, KID.
SHIT.
BRODSKY.
HOW DID HE -- ?
MAYA?
OH, DON'T GO BLAMIN' THE GIRL...
YOU'RE THE MORON WHO LEFT A DEAD BODY PARKED IN FRONT OF HER HOUSE.
SHE'S JUST DOING WHAT SHE'S TOLD TO... LIKE ALWAYS.
FINE... THE HELL WITH IT, YOU SON OF A BITCH...

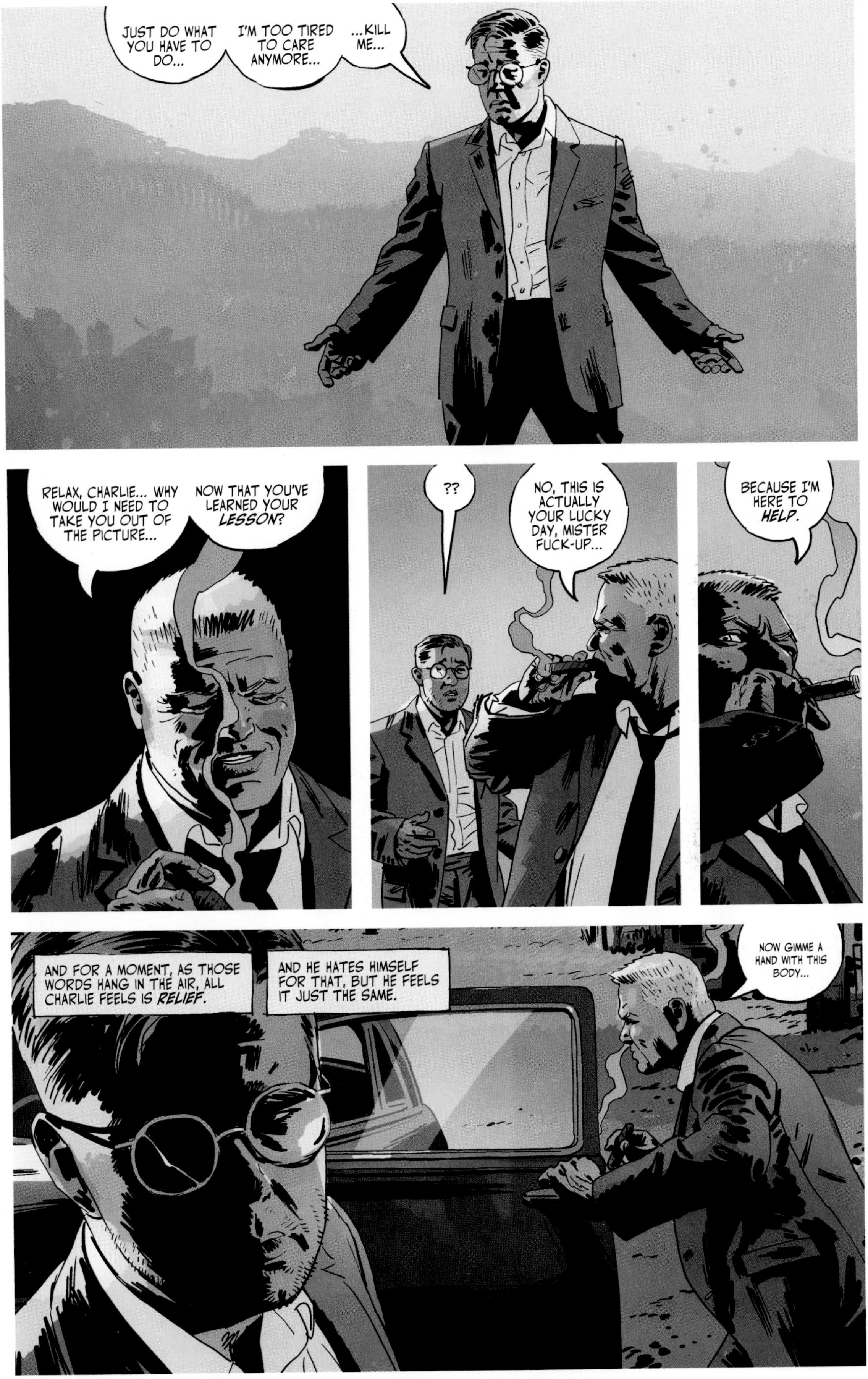
JUST DO WHAT YOU HAVE TO DO...
I'M TOO TIRED TO CARE ANYMORE...
...KILL ME...
RELAX, CHARLIE... WHY WOULD I NEED TO TAKE YOU OUT OF THE PICTURE...
NOW THAT YOU'VE LEARNED YOUR LESSON?
??
NO, THIS IS ACTUALLY YOUR LUCKY DAY, MISTER FUCK-UP...
BECAUSE I'M HERE TO HELP.
AND FOR A MOMENT, AS THOSE WORDS HANG IN THE AIR, ALL CHARLIE FEELS IS RELIEF.
AND HE HATES HIMSELF FOR THAT, BUT HE FEELS IT JUST THE SAME.
NOW GIMME A HAND WITH THIS BODY...

Six Weeks Later

WAKE UP, UNCLE CHARLIE...

...FFUHH...

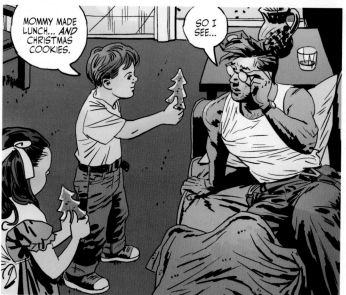

MOMMY MADE LUNCH... AND CHRISTMAS COOKIES.

SO I SEE...

ISN'T THAT GOING TO SPOIL YOUR APPETITE?

DON'T BE SILLY, UNCLE CHARLIE.

WHAT'S HE TALKING ABOUT? HOW COULD COOKIES SPOIL ANYTHING?

DON'T LISTEN TO HIM, JIMMY, HE'S CRAZY...

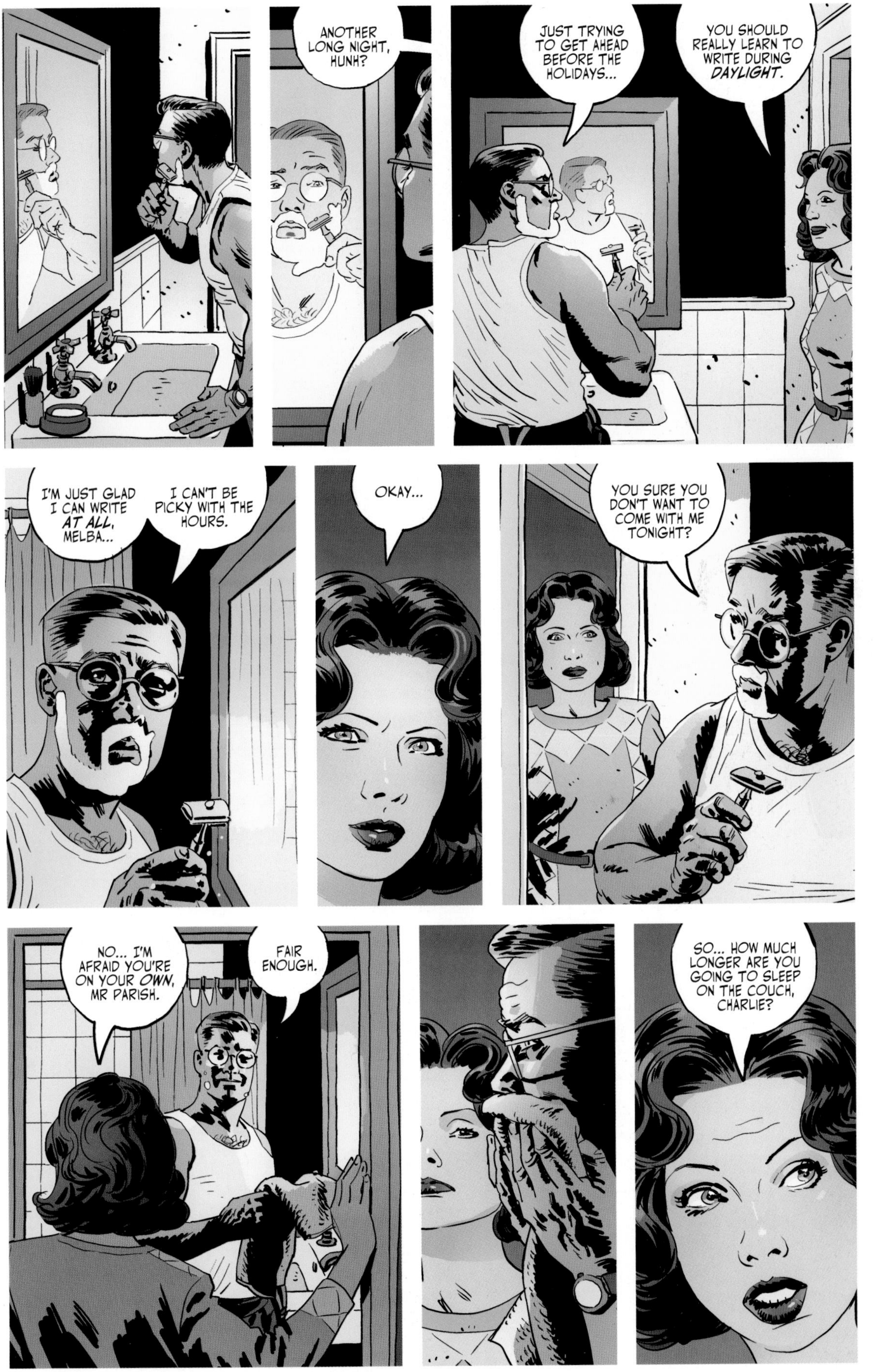
ANOTHER LONG NIGHT, HUNH?
JUST TRYING TO GET AHEAD BEFORE THE HOLIDAYS...
YOU SHOULD REALLY LEARN TO WRITE DURING *DAYLIGHT*.
I'M JUST GLAD I CAN WRITE *AT ALL*, MELBA...
I CAN'T BE PICKY WITH THE HOURS.
OKAY...
YOU SURE YOU DON'T WANT TO COME WITH ME TONIGHT?
NO... I'M AFRAID YOU'RE ON YOUR *OWN*, MR PARISH.
FAIR ENOUGH.
SO... HOW MUCH LONGER ARE YOU GOING TO SLEEP ON THE COUCH, CHARLIE?

I'M NOT SURE.

WELL, DON'T TAKE *FOREVER* TO MAKE UP YOUR MIND...

I MIGHT START TAKING IT PERSONALLY.

A FEW NIGHTS AFTER GIL'S FUNERAL, MELBA HAD BROUGHT CHARLIE INTO HER ROOM...

SHE WANTED TO BE HELD... TO FEEL ALIVE...

AND CHARLIE HAD FELT THE SAME WAY.

BUT IN THE MORNING, HE COULDN'T LOOK AT HIMSELF.

GIL WOULDN'T HAVE CARED... HE WOULD HAVE *APPROVED*, EVEN, MELBA WOULD SAY...

BUT CHARLIE HAD STAYED ON THE COUCH SINCE THEN.

THE OFFICIAL STORY WAS *GAMBLING DEBTS*. GIL'S BODY HAD BEEN "FOUND" IN THE DESERT, WHERE SEVERAL *MOB VICTIMS* HAD BEEN DUMPED OVER THE YEARS.

IT ADDED UP AND NO ONE LOOKED ANY DEEPER.

MELBA WAS HEARTBROKEN, BUT CHARLIE SAW THERE WAS SOMETHING *ELSE* IN HER, TOO...

LIKE THE *INEVITABLE* HAD HAPPENED AND SHE COULD FINALLY STOP *WAITING* FOR IT.

HE WASN'T SURE IF THAT MADE HIM FEEL BETTER OR *WORSE* ABOUT LYING TO HER...

BUT THE LIE HAD ALLOWED LIFE TO GO ON, AT LEAST.

AND MOST DAYS...

THAT WAS NO SMALL CONSOLATION.

TYLER GRAVES AND MAYA SILVER HAD RECENTLY GOTTEN *ENGAGED*...

AND THE *PREMIERE* WAS THEIR FIRST *PUBLIC APPEARANCE* SINCE THE NEWS HAD LEAKED.

IT WAS A SMART *PR* MOVE... MAKING SURE THE PRESS WOULD BE FOCUSED ON *MAYA*...

AND NOT THE GIRL SHE HAD REPLACED.

THE ONE WHO WAS *SUPPOSED* TO BE IN THE SPOTLIGHT TONIGHT.

NICE *ROCK*, HUH?

I DON'T KNOW DIAMONDS, BUT IT'S *BIG*...

HOW MUCH DID THE STUDIO PAY FOR IT?

YOU DON'T WANT TO KNOW, CHARLIE.

REALLY? *THAT* MUCH?

OBSCENE.

HEY, SPEAKING OF OBSCENE... *EARL* WAS LOOKING FOR YOU.

BUT I THINK HE ALREADY WENT INSIDE.

THANKS. YOU WANT TO –

OH GOD... NO... LOUELLA PARSONS IS TALKING TO *TYLER*...

I'LL SEE YOU IN THERE.

SEEYA, DOTTIE...

...DAMMIT...

DON'T LOOK SO GLUM, PARISH...

...IT AIN'T A *REAL* MARRIAGE.

I CAN STILL GET HER TO GO BACK TO *SCREWING* YOU, IF YOU WANT.

THOUGH *WHY* YOU'D WANT TO SCREW A *MEXICAN* FULL-TIME...

YOU'RE A *PIG,* BRODSKY.

EASY, PAL... DON'T WANNA HAVE TO REPORT BACK TO *MR THURSBY* THAT YOU'RE ACTING-UP...

NOT AFTER EVERYTHING THE STUDIO'S *DONE* FOR YOU.

I'M NOT *ACTING-UP...* JUST...

STOP BEING AN ASSHOLE...

SO... THE *BIG BOSS* ISN'T COMING TO THE PREMIERE?

NAHH...

"HE'S BACK AT THE LOT, WATCHING HIS OWN *CUT* OF THIS PICTURE.

"VAL SOMMERS MEANT *TOO MUCH* TO THE OLD MAN..."

"SAID HE COULDN'T WATCH HER GET *PAINTED-OVER* LIKE THIS."

PERSONALLY, I NEVER SAW ANYTHING *SPECIAL* IN VAL, BUT --

I SAID TO *STOP* BEING AN ASSHOLE.

I'M NOT AN ASSHOLE, I'M A FUCKIN' REALIST.

AND YOU ARE, TOO, UNDERNEATH ALL YOUR BULLSHIT...

I'VE SEEN YOUR *MILITARY FILE.*

SHUT UP.

WHAT I'M *SAYIN'* IS, YOU KNOW JUSTICE IS A GODDAM FAIRY TALE.

THAT'S WHY YOU DIDN'T CALL THE *COPS* WHEN YOU FOUND THE GIRL'S BODY...

AND THAT'S WHY I KNOW YOU'RE GONNA LEARN TO *LIVE* WITH THIS.

ANYWAY, THEY'RE STARTING THE PICTURE... I'LL SEE YOU AT THE *AFTER-PARTY*...

WAIT.

MAYBE I *CAN* LEARN TO LIVE WITH IT...

BUT NOT WITHOUT *KNOWING.*

WHO SAYS I KNOW? I'M PAID TO *FORGET* THINGS.

JUST TELL ME WHAT *HAPPENED* THAT NIGHT, PHIL...

JUST *FUCKING* TELL ME.

YOU THINK ANYTHING I SAY IS GONNA MAKE YOU FEEL *BETTER?*

NOT ONE BIT.

OKAY THEN... BUT NOT HERE...

LET'S SAY *MAYBE*...

MAYBE *WHAT?*

MAYBE, MEANIN' I WASN'T THERE... AND PEOPLE LIKE TO *LIE* ABOUT DEAD BODIES.

SO I CAN'T TELL YOU WHAT HAPPENED, CHARLIE...

BUT I CAN TELL YOU WHAT *MIGHT'VE.*

"SEE, MAYBE THERE'S THIS GUY, THIS *G-MAN* POSING AS A PRODUCER...

"HE'S HERE HUNTIN' *COMMIES*, BUT HE'S ALSO SUPPOSED TO BLEND IN...

"AND MAYBE THAT'S WHERE A GUY LIKE THIS GETS INTO *TROUBLE.*

"HE STARTS *ENJOYING* HIS NEW LIFE TOO MUCH.

"THE PARTIES, THE ACTRESSES... THAT'S ENOUGH TO TWIST MOST PRODUCERS' MINDS..."

BUT THIS GUY'S GOT A KIND OF POWER *REAL PRODUCERS* DON'T.

HE'S DIGGIN' UP DIRT AND USING IT TO GET 'EM ALL TO TURN ON EACH OTHER.

DON'T WANT THE PRESS TO HEAR YOU HAD AN ABORTION? THEN YOU BETTER *NAME* SOME REDS.

"DON'T HAVE ANY NAMES TO GIVE?

"WELL THEN, THERE'S *OTHER WAYS* TO PAY HIM OFF."

AFTER A WHILE, HE'S LIKE THE WORST OF BOTH WORLDS... THE FEDS *AND* THE STUDIO BOSSES...

RUTHLESS, GREEDY, PARANOID...

VINDICTIVE.

AND SO THIS GUY... MAYBE HE THINKS HE'S *GOT* SOMETHING ON OLD MAN THURSBY...

A WAY TO PUT THE WHOLE *STUDIO* UNDER J. EDGAR'S THUMB.

BUT FOR IT TO WORK, HE NEEDS VAL SOMMERS TO GIVE HIM SOME KINDA EVIDENCE.

"ONLY SHE WON'T GIVE UP ANYTHING... NOT ON THURSBY *OR* THE STUDIO... NOTHING...

"SO THE GUY JUST *CRACKS*... MAYBE.

"HE CAN'T STAND IT...

"THAT HIS POWER DOESN'T *WORK* ON HER.

"AND MAYBE AFTER HE'S DONE WITH HER, WITH EVERYTHING, HE CALLS LOOKIN' FOR HELP... ALL BUSTED-UP..."

WHY WOULDN'T SHE JUST GIVE ME A *NAME?* ANYBODY...

"LIKE IT'S HER FAULT HE'S GOT IT *WRONG* ABOUT THURSBY..."

"LIKE IT'S HER FAULT SHE DIDN'T HAVE ANY *COMMIES* TO GIVE UP..."

YEAH... RIGHT...

AND THE KICKER IS, I CAN'T EVEN *KILL* THIS GUY FOR WHAT HE MAYBE DONE.

BECAUSE HE'S *FBI.*

YEAH... *MAYBE.*

I MEAN, WE'RE JUST *SPECULATING* HERE.

BUT THAT *IS* HOW IT WORKS, CHARLIE. GIRLS DIE FOR NOTHIN' AND OLD MEN CRY ABOUT IT...

AND THE BUSINESS JUST *KEEPS* ON GOING...

CHRISTMAS STILL COMES *EVERY GODDAM YEAR,* RIGHT ON SCHEDULE...

BRODSKY'S TALKING ABOUT HOW *ALIKE* THEY ARE... HOW THEY BOTH UNDERSTAND THE WORLD...

WHEN CHARLIE GRABS THE WHISKEY AND WANDERS OUT INTO THE STREET...

THEY'RE STILL LINED-UP OUTSIDE THE PREMIERE, ALL THOSE DESPERATE FACES...

THEIR EYES FIXED ON HIM, ACCUSING...

WHY DIDN'T VAL GIVE YOU UP, CHARLIE?

WHY DID SHE DIE WITH YOUR SECRET LOCKED INSIDE HER?

THERE'S A BUZZING IN HIS HEAD... AND IT MAKES HIM THINK ABOUT THE *PHANTOM PLANES* AGAIN.

THAT NIGHT AFTER PEARL HARBOR, WHEN EVERYONE HEARD *JAPANESE BOMBERS* OVERHEAD... BUT HE DIDN'T...

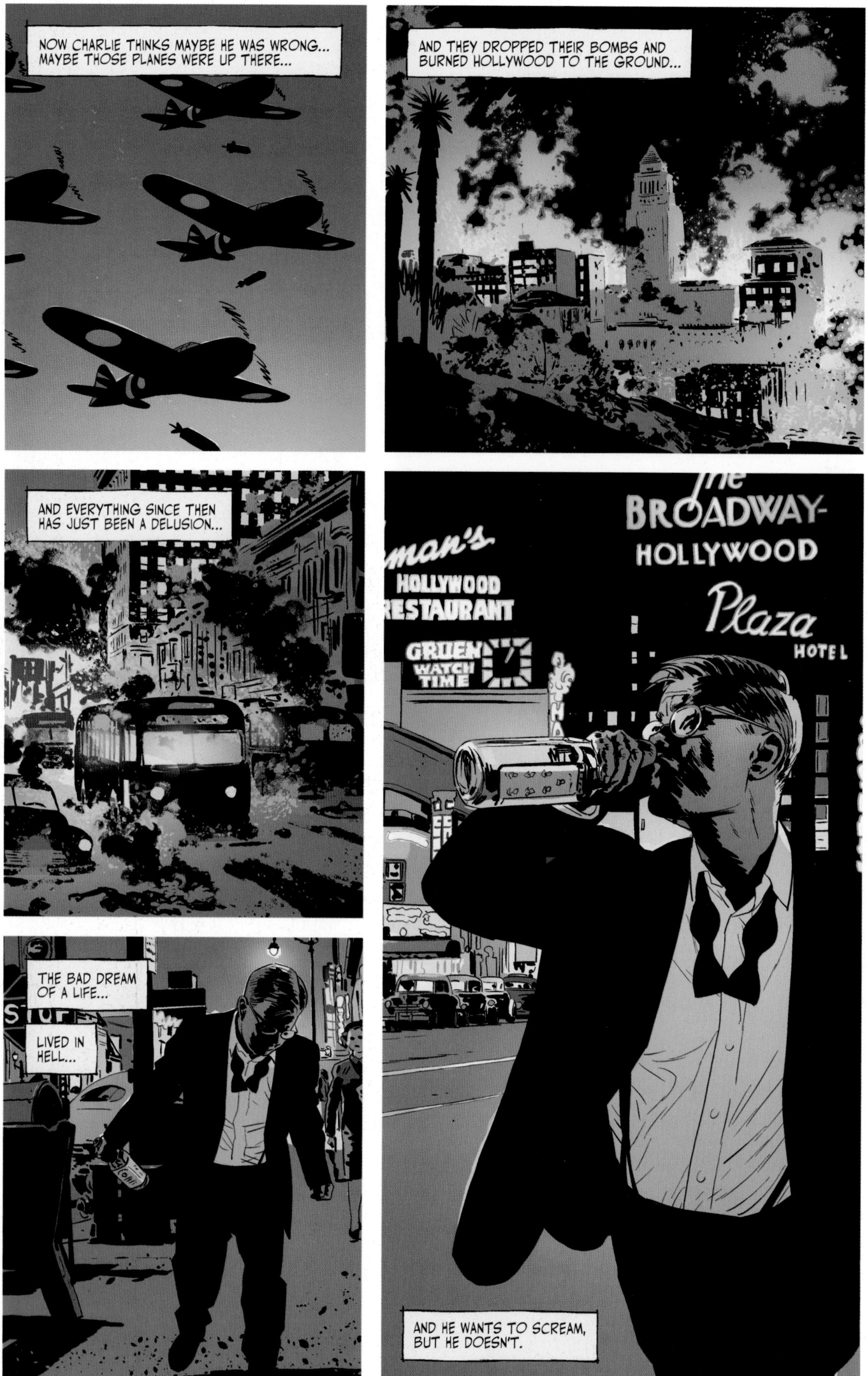
NOW CHARLIE THINKS MAYBE HE WAS WRONG... MAYBE THOSE PLANES WERE UP THERE...
AND THEY DROPPED THEIR BOMBS AND BURNED HOLLYWOOD TO THE GROUND...
AND EVERYTHING SINCE THEN HAS JUST BEEN A DELUSION...
THE BROADWAY-HOLLYWOOD
HOLLYWOOD RESTAURANT
GRUEN WATCH TIME
Plaza HOTEL
THE BAD DREAM OF A LIFE...
LIVED IN HELL...
AND HE WANTS TO SCREAM, BUT HE DOESN'T.

Screen Views and News

'Shadow of the Valley' – Earl Rath's Dark Journey!

By Eileen Theo

"Shadow of the Valley" the new thriller at the Palace—and what a thrill it is!—is a revelation for two reasons. First, because for the first time in his dashing career as a leading man, Earl Rath steps out from under the shadow of Fairbanks and Flynn who he's long been compared to, and shows a riveting dark side none of his charm and good-looks have ever hinted at before. Both the ladies and gents will leave the theater with chills. I dare say! And what is the second revelation of this "accused-murderer-on-the-run" picture? Dazzling new starlet, Maya Silver, whose performance held a gravity and depth far beyond the dialog her character, Gracie, was given to speak. There's something deep and haunted inside this young dancer-turned-actress, and her mysterious beauty has all of Hollywood abuzz.

"Shadow of the Valley" comes from a short story originally published in Black Mask by legendary writer Jacob Thacke whose work was rediscov following his death in

The covers from original serialization

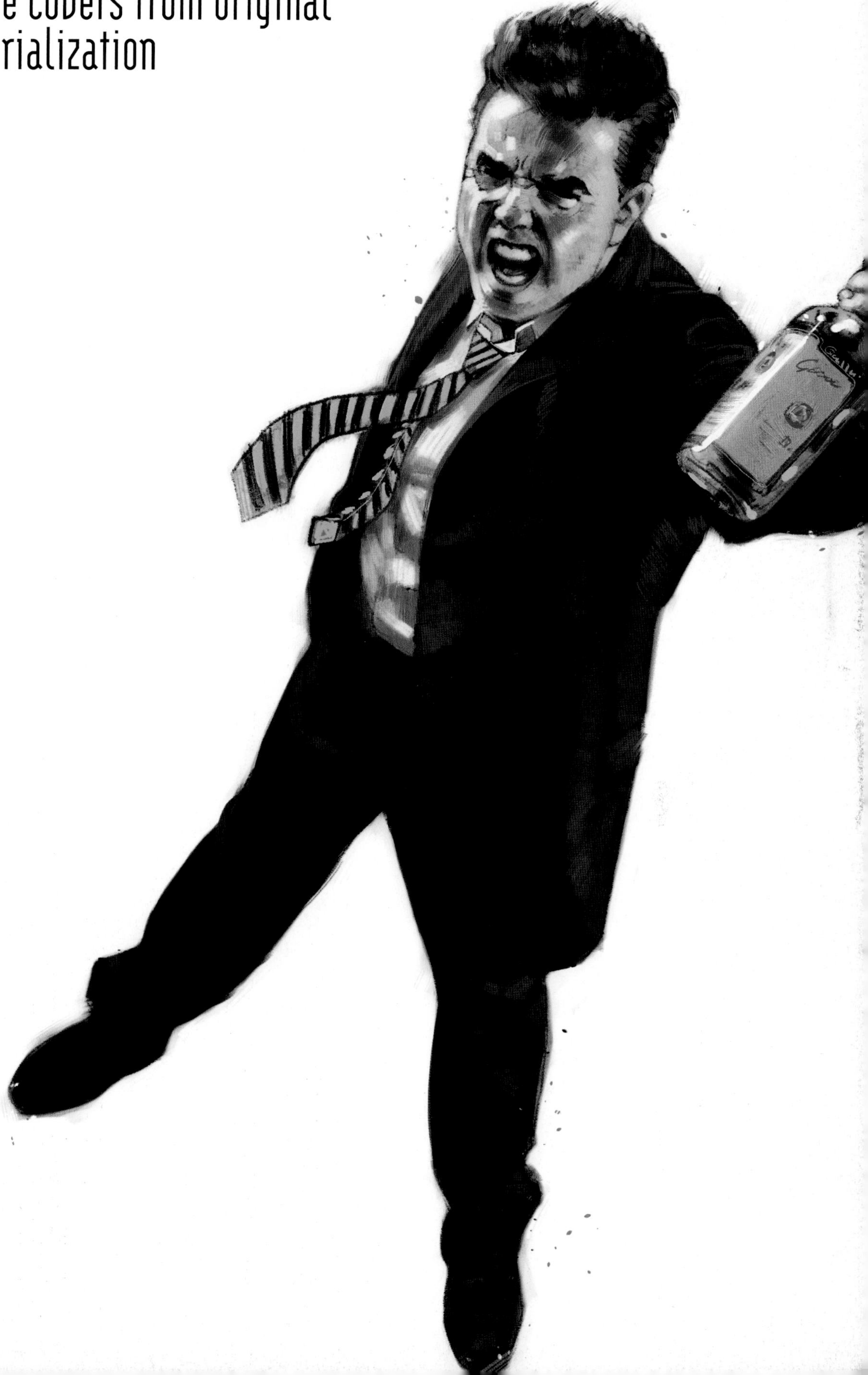

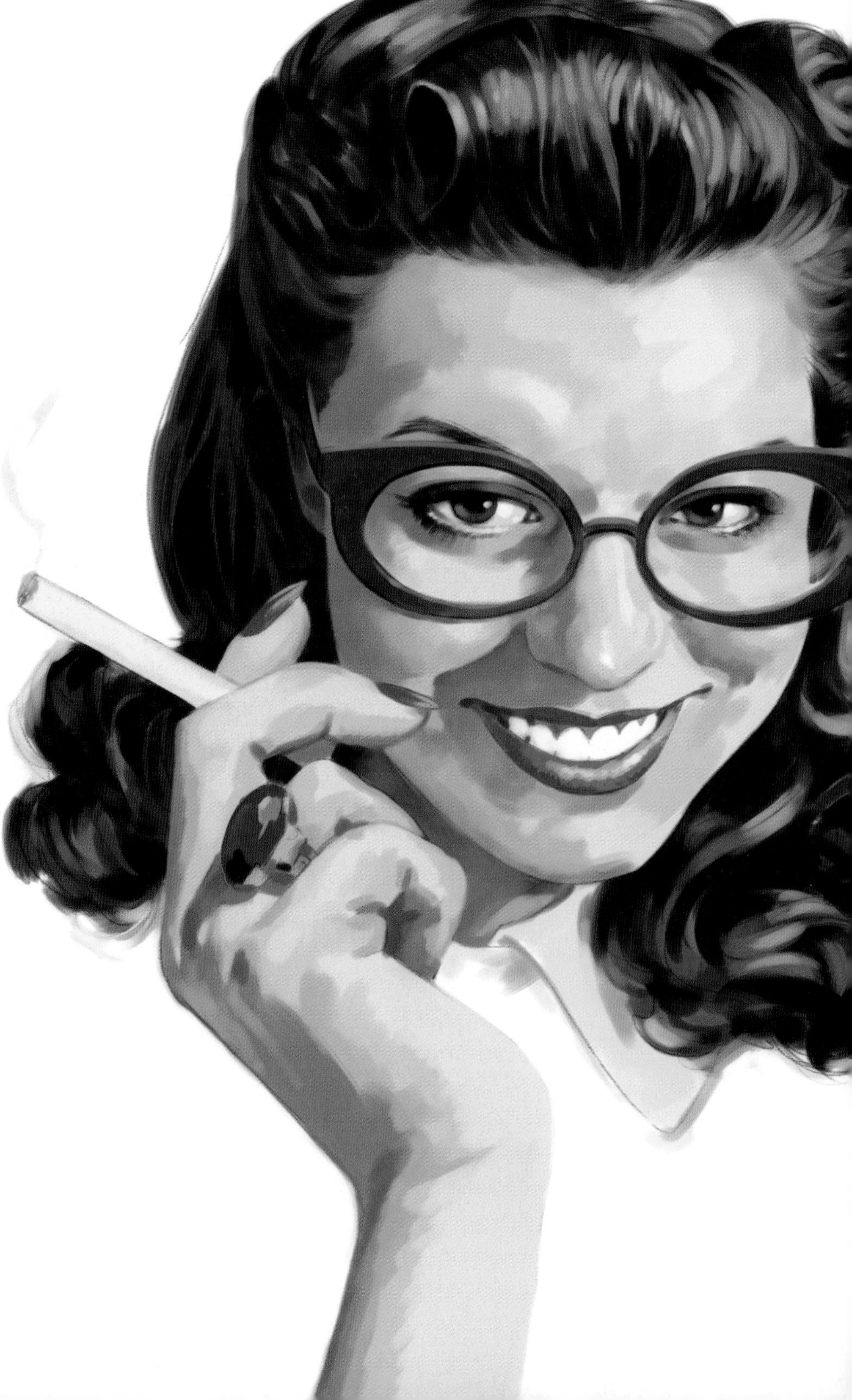

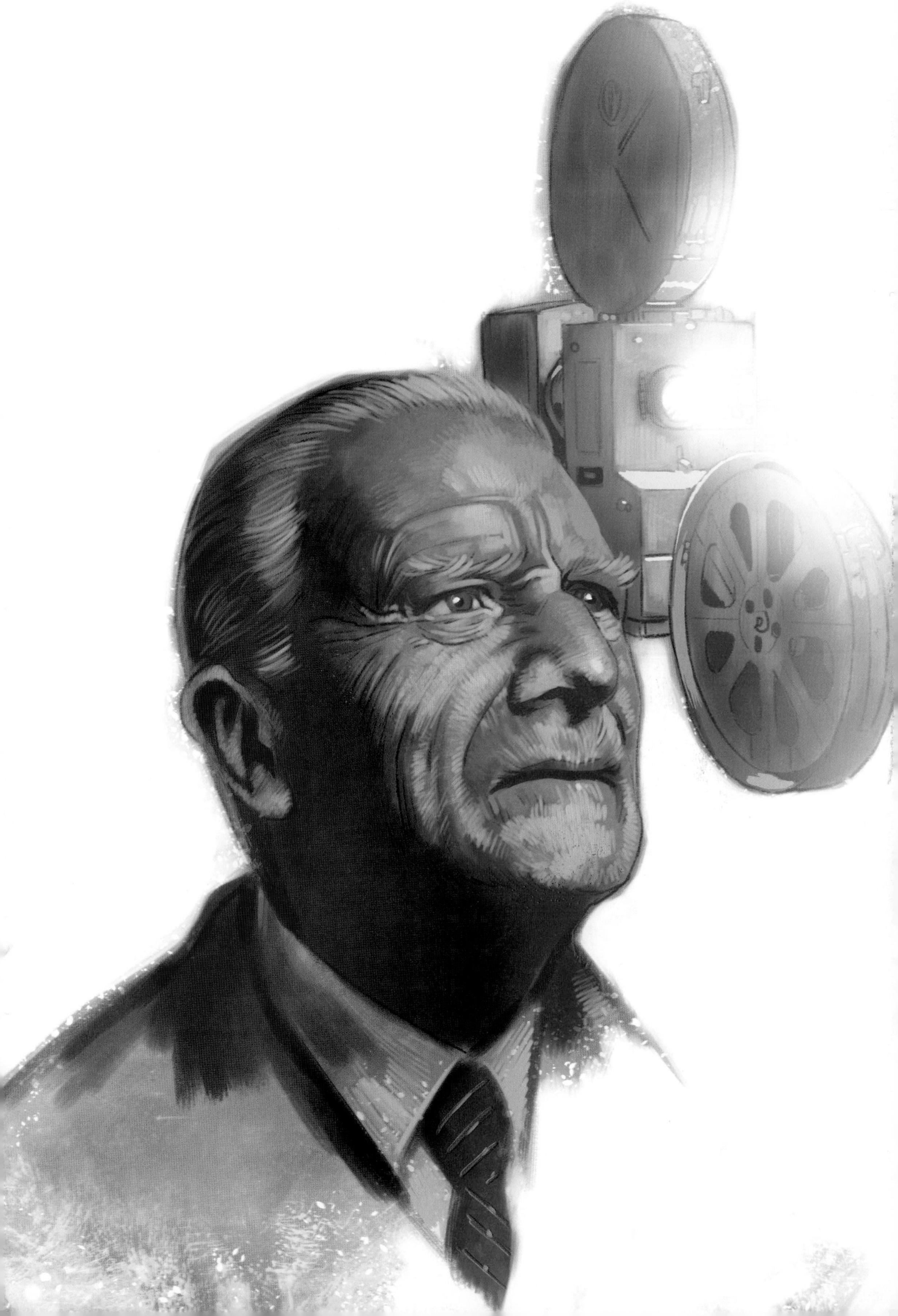

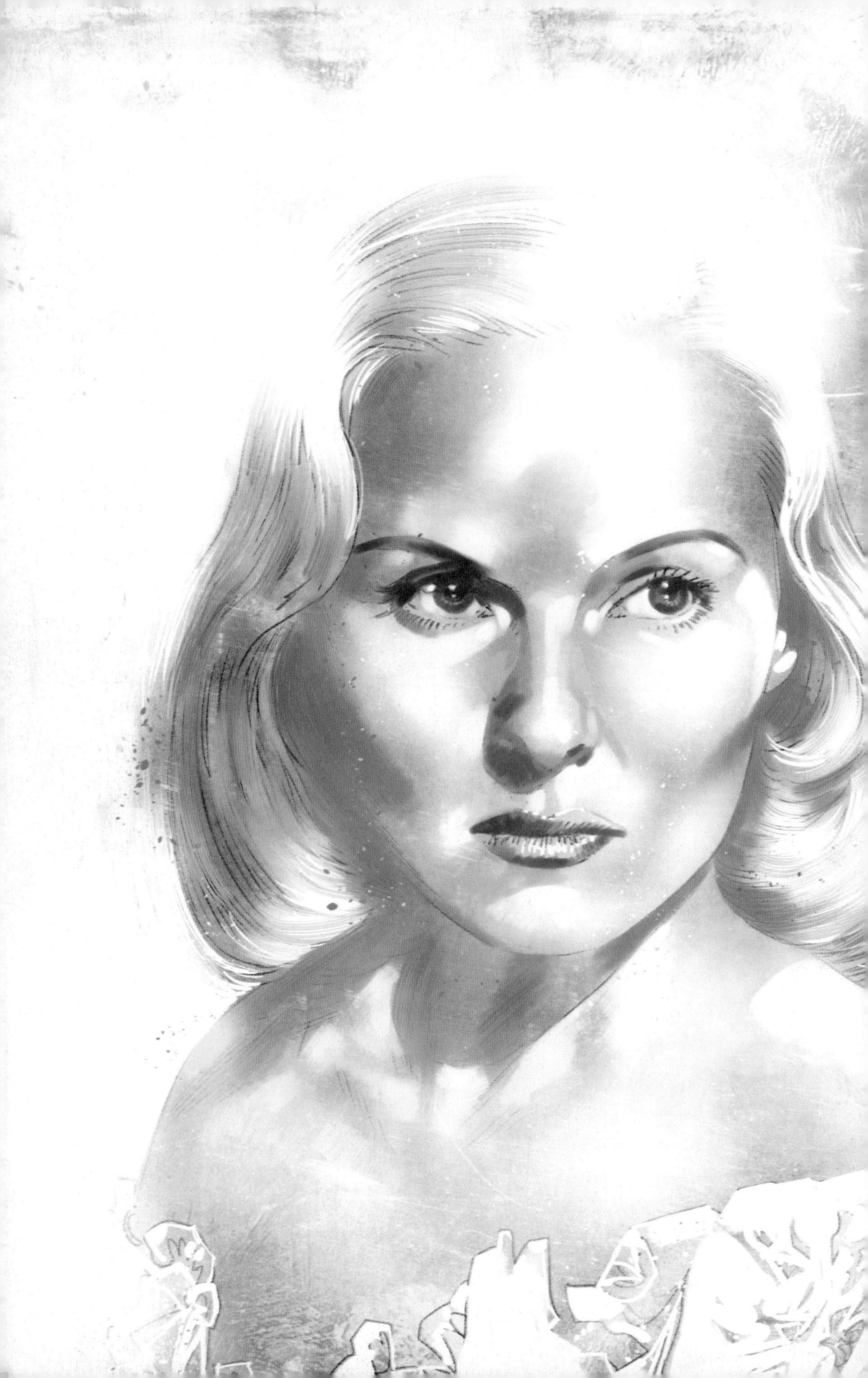